Learning and Language
in the
Classroom

*Discursive talking and
writing across the curriculum*

Other Pergamon titles of interest

BARON G.
The Politics of School Government

BOUCHER L.
Tradition and Change in Swedish Education

McGUIRE J. & PRIESTLEY P.
Life After School

ROSS M.
The Aesthetic Imperative: Relevance and Responsibility
in Arts Education
The Arts and Personal Growth
The Development of Aesthetic Experience

A Related Pergamon Journal

LANGUAGE & COMMUNICATION*
An Interdisciplinary Journal

Editor: Roy Harris, *University of Oxford*

The primary aim of the journal is to fill the need for a publication forum devoted to the discussion of topics and issues in communication which are of interdisciplinary significance. It will publish contributions from researchers in all fields relevant to the study of verbal and non-verbal communication.

Emphasis will be placed on the implication of current research for establishing common theoretical frameworks within which findings from different areas of study may be accommodated and interrelated.

By focusing attention on the many ways in which language is integrated with other forms of communicational activity and interactional behaviour it is intended to explore ways of developing a science of communication which is not restricted by existing disciplinary boundaries.

*Free specimen copy available on request.

Learning and Language
in the
Classroom

Discursive talking and
writing across the curriculum

by
PETER CHILVER
and
GERARD GOULD

PERGAMON PRESS

OXFORD · NEW YORK · TORONTO · SYDNEY · PARIS · FRANKFURT

U.K.	Pergamon Press Ltd., Headington Hill Hall, Oxford OX3 0BW, England
U.S.A.	Pergamon Press Inc., Maxwell House, Fairview Park, Elmsford, New York 10523, U.S.A.
CANADA	Pergamon Press Canada Ltd., Suite 104, 150 Consumers Rd., Willowdale, Ontario M2J 1P9, Canada
AUSTRALIA	Pergamon Press (Aust.) Pty. Ltd., P.O. Box 544, Potts Point, N.S.W. 2011, Australia
FRANCE	Pergamon Press SARL, 24 rue des Ecoles, 75240 Paris, Cedex 05, France
FEDERAL REPUBLIC OF GERMANY	Pergamon Press GmbH, 6242 Kronberg-Taunus, Hammerweg 6, Federal Republic of Germany

First edition 1982

Library of Congress Cataloguing in Publication Data

Chilver, Peter.
Learning and language in the classroom.
Includes bibliographical references and
index.
1. Language arts (Elementary) 2. Forums
(Discussion and debate) 3. Education,
Elementary—Curricula. I. Gould, Gerard.
II. Title.
LB1576.C5535   1982   372.6   82-527

British Library Cataloguing in Publication Data

Chilver, Peter
Learning and language in the classroom.
1. Learning, Psychology of
2. Children—Language
I. Title II. Gould, Gerard
370.15'23   LB1139.L3
ISBN 0-08-026777-7

Printed and Bound in Great Britain by
Redwood Burn Limited, Trowbridge, Wiltshire.

Contents

3.   Group Discussion: The Teacher's Role   **46**

4.   Class Discussion: The Teacher's Role   **51**

5.   Reading: Group Discussion of a Passage   **63**

Introduction

It will be helpful to spell out from the beginning the kind of book we have attempted to write, and the procedures we have followed.

Purpose

This is a book by teachers and for teachers, and it is concerned with the various ways in which children are taught and with the various ways in which they learn in response to that teaching. We have ourselves been teaching for many years - for roughly half a century in fact, if we add together our two careers - and we have worked at almost every educational level, including primary and secondary schools (of various kinds) and various colleges. And we have also taught, in one way or another, a fair range of subjects, from English and drama to law and modern languages. Like all teachers we have been caught up in the exciting and frustrating dilemma of how to understand better what we do and how we do it, and like many of our colleagues, have been especially interested in the rapid growth of a virtually new body of learning, over the last dozen years or so, concerned with the role of language in learning. One practical result of this new body of knowledge, especially as it reflected itself in the *Bullock Report*, has been a new concern with the underlying connections between the work of all teachers and all subjects, and hence with language policies across the curriculum. The *Bullock Report* made a special point of the need for teachers in the school (and in different schools) to come together to start to compare their procedures, their expectations and their problems, and this book is simply a contribution to such discussions. It is intended for all teachers, of all subjects, at all points in the curriculum of the schools.

Assumptions

Our work is based on a number of assumptions. *Children want to learn.* Despite the generally depressed image of schools, teachers and pupils that is handed on by the media (including the work of novelists and film-makers as well as of journalists) children are immensely keen to add to their experience, to make more sense of the world, to transcend themselves. One of the most interesting illustrations of this occurred a few years ago when one of the two writers was engaged to run a summer school for local children in West London. It was financed in part by a Home Office grant, subsequently withdrawn, for supporting measures which helped to bring together immigrant and native children at a time when, otherwise, racial conflict might well be festering. The project was organized through a teacher-training college which in its turn provided a large number of enthusiastic student-teachers. But their enthusiasm was hardly a match for that of the children themselves. Not only did we have to turn away applicants, daily; what was more surprising was the curriculum itself. In planning our summer school we had deliberately invited the children to think about and then to suggest the kind of summer school they wanted - which was, of course, in the summer holidays. A great range of ideas came out of this, almost all of which, technically, we were able to accommodate. They included such things as learning to play the guitar, swimming, and typing. But the most widely popular classes were those in what we would loosely call 'conventional' school subjects or activities, such as mathematics, writing (for example, preparing a magazine), and foreign languages. There was, in other words, an immense desire and willingness to spend 'free' time, voluntarily, to supplement and extend the work already being explored in the schools themselves. Children want to learn.

What children learn is fundamentally related to what they are taught and how they are taught. As an example, if we teach children not to think about history, or mathematics, or science, then they tend not to think about them. If we teach them to 'memorize the facts' then they memorize the facts, and so on. Of course, children are active, not passive learners, and they bring to their work a complex storehouse of experience that is unique to each child and from which each child ventures forth to the new experiences offered in a classroom. But within children's successes and failures, total or relative, the imprint of their teaching is generally clear. A third and final assumption follows from this.

Whatever a child does as part of the learning-teaching process *is automatically of importance and significance to teachers.* It is only in fairly recent years that teachers at in-service courses and training programmes have become used to looking at actual examples of children's work-in-progress, but it is still not uncommon to hear such work dismissed with the simple verdict that no good teacher would elicit such work in the first place. Such a procedure, of course, rules out any possibility of seeing whether or not the child is doing anything useful, or of seeing - and this is perhaps more to the point - where the child's difficulties happen to lie. Everything depends, though, on teachers having a number of different ways of looking at such work, and it is one such way that we are keen to promote in this book. In a very basic sense, the 'truth' about any teaching lies not in the procedures of the teacher, whether we are talking about the teacher's methods, techniques or philosophical aims, but in the responses of the child. Hence an intrinsic and positive interest in the work of the child, in *everything the child does,* and not merely in what the child appears to do well or successfully, is a fundamental part of learning to teach. And we see this as the task of a lifetime!

Discursive Talking and Writing

Our particular focus throughout the book is on discursive talk and discursive writing across the curriculum. By *discursive* talk we mean talk which seeks to explore ideas carefully and conscientiously; to think things through; to consider possible answers to questions and problems. And similarly with discursive writing.

The discursive use of language is an important part of any school curriculum, but not the only part. *Informative* language, which seeks in various ways to represent and report rather than to discuss and evaluate, also plays an important part. So, too, does *persuasive* language, where the emphasis is upon seeking to affect the outcome of events. So, too, does *creative* language, as with the creating of a poem or play. Such categories of language do not, of course, in any sense exhaust the language of the curriculum. Nor are they mutually exclusive. Discursiveness is a part of creativity; discursiveness is impossible without information; and so on. But our focus here is on discursiveness primarily. Other uses of language are explored occasionally for contrast and illumination.

Talking, Reading and Writing

Learning to write discursively is also a matter of learning to talk discursively, and both are related to learning to read an increasing diversity of literature. Hence, the major part of the book is devoted to examples of children *talking,* whether as a small group or as a class, and to them talking about what they are *reading,* to them *making notes,* and to them *writing.*

We have collected examples of these activities from quite a fair range of subjects and from children aged 11 to 16. But we must stress that we have not even attempted to collect perfect examples of such activities, even if perfection is possible. Very simply, all the work that we use by way of illustration has some claim to be considered discursive and hence to be evaluated as such.

Outline of the book

It will be helpful to spell out in advance the general line and development of our ideas:

Chapter 1

Chapter 1 looks at a group of 16-year-olds discussing their ideas for the writing of a history essay. We use their discussion to draw out an underlying structure which we later use to evaluate other discursive activities (in class discussion, reading and writing). In this structure, we suggest there are four interrelated factors at work:

1. The ways in which the participants think about their task;
2. The knowledge they employ;
3. The ways in which they work;
4. The language they use.

Chapter 2

Chapter 2 takes this structure or model, and looking at a range of different subjects and activities, suggests some of the specific problems which arise in discursive work of all kinds. These are in relation to: *ways of thinking* about a task - the conflicting demands of economy and precision, of correctness and creativity, and of relating the parts to the whole and the whole to the parts; *knowledge employed* - problems can emanate from the different assumptions the learner makes and the assumptions made by the teacher, and these in turn affect the learner's sense of what is and what is not relevant to the tasks; *ways of working* - problems can emanate from a lack of models of how to work, a lack of variety in the kinds of work, and a lack of preliminary work (making rough notes for instance); *language used* - problems can emanate from an unfamiliarity with the appropriate register and hence from a lack of linguistic models, or from the complexity of the language itself, or from a confusion as to the kind of linguistic difficulty involved.

Chapter 3 and 4

Chapters 3 and 4 look at the teacher's role, first in group discussion, and then in class discussion, using the same model to outline the contribution of the teacher to the children's learning.

Chapters 5 and 6

Chapters 5 and 6 look at reading across the curriculum. First we look at a small group of children discussing a prose passage (in science) and then at a small group of children discussing a cloze comprehension test. We then outline the teacher's role in the development of children's reading.

Chapter 7

Chapter 7 briefly explores the teacher's role in helping children to make useful notes.

Chapters 8 and 9

The final section of the book looks at the teacher's role in the development of children's writing. We begin by looking at children writing stories, partly because this offers some scope for comparison with discursive writing, partly because story-writing is the most common form of writing used in the curriculum. Chapter 8 looks at story-writing, Chapter 9 looks at discursive writing. The examples we offer are all drawn from the work of one pupil, writing across the curriculum, and they represent each year's work, from age 11 to age 16.

In our conclusion we draw together the different discursive activities of talking, reading and writing in relation to the development of the child and the work of the teacher. In our thinking we are drawing upon a great range of different sources. Since we are keen to hold on to our own line of thought we do not necessarily indicate these in the text, but we spell them out briefly in the notes at the end of the book.

1

Language in Use: Analyzing a Group Discussion

Introduction

Our initial need is for a way of looking at all kinds of language activity, regardless of subject-matter, so that we can use it not only for describing and evaluating what is happening within an individual subject, but also for comparing what is happening across subject boundaries. In other words, we need a model of language in use, a grid, as it were, that we can fit over a whole range of subjects and activities to help us to explore more fully what is happening. We can then begin to compare, for example, the work of a group of children engaged in a discussion, with the work of a group of children reading or writing.

In this chapter we put forward a particular way of analyzing what happens in one specific activity - a group discussion. In later chapters, we use the same analysis as a way of interpreting what happens elsewhere in the curriculum.

The word 'talking' is a vast umbrella under which can be brought together activities as diverse as lecturing, story-telling, gossip, incidental chat while doing something else, and talking together about some problem in a detached but friendly fashion. All kinds of talk have a place in the curriculum, but it is the idea of *talking together about a problem* that we wish to explore here, partly because it is so little practised anywhere, whether in school or outside, and also because it has such immense potential as a way of learning and hence of teaching.

Class discussion is equally important, but we feel that it is a basically different activity from a group discussion, and the two are worth looking at separately.

What Happens in a Group Discussion? What Are Its Essential Features?

What follows is an attempt to answer these questions, using as the basis for our suggestions, the transcript of a peer group of five boys, aged 16, talking about a problem in history. We are not claiming that this is a perfect discussion, or that it is *purely* a discussion. To the contrary, all discussion constantly overlaps with other things, such as gossip and drama. It is simply that this particular discussion shows what seems to us to be the fundamental shape, including the problems and limitations, of all discussion. Finally, it must be stressed that we are also not in any sense arguing that children younger than these could not achieve the formal standards of this particular example. To the contrary, we think that all children and all adults can and do engage in such discussion when they have a number of appropriate opportunities - including the chance simply to try their hands at doing so.

Planning a History Essay: Group of 16-year-olds

There is no teacher present. They have been given the essay title just before the discussion starts, having previously worked on the topic in class. They have a single copy of a history text-book with them, which they can use if they wish. They are friends and have quite often worked in this way as a group. They are a self-chosen group. They have agreed to tape-record their conversation. Their names are Andrew, Harry, John, Mark and Philip.

The title of the essay is:
Outline the Course of American Influence in Cuba
From World War I to the Present Day

The Group Discussion

Harry:	*So we've got to do an essay.*
John:	*Yeah.*
Harry:	*So we start off with a bit of background then. When did America get any interest in Cuba from the beginning?*
Philip:	*About the beginning of the nineteenth century. . . .* (5)
Harry:	*Yeah, the Cuban struggle for independence. It was under Spanish control. The Spanish-American War was it? (Yeah) At the end of the nineteenth century.*
John:	*Yeah.*
Harry:	*Did they control. . .?* (10)
Philip:	*Till Fidel Castro overthrew. . .*
Harry:	*Wait a minute! Now we're going into the 1960s. When did they intervene in Cuba?*
John:	*(Looking up information in text-book) Something about 1900 to the 1930s* (15)
Harry:	*Why did they intervene in Cuba in 1912 and that?*
John:	*When did Batista come to power?*
Philip:	*1933.*
John:	*The Americans put him there. Then during the 50s he*

became a tyrant to the country, so the Americans cut off (20)
their supplies.

Harry: *Did they support Castro?*
John: *Yeah. They encouraged a resistance movement.*
Harry: *In the 50s?*
John: *Drawing to the 60s. They started supplying Castro with* (25)
          arms.
Harry: *Who was the President then? Eisenhower?*
Philip: *Yeah.*
Harry: *When did he come in?*
John: *1956* (30)
Harry: *Who was before him?*
John: *Truman?*
Harry: *So, it was Truman and Eisenhower. What were they -*
          Democratic?
John: *Yeah.* (35)
Harry: *I thought Eisenhower was Republican. I'm not sure. I'm*
          not sure.
John: *I'll look it up.*
Harry: *So they supported Castro. Shall we put in a bit about*
          Castro? (40)
John: *He started up his group in the highlands or whatever it*
          was.
Philip: *The mountains.*
John: *Yeah, the mountains of Cuba. He started up. Then the*
          American resistance against Cuba. So his movement (45)
          started building up towards a more greater. . . .
Harry: *Shall we put in anything about Castro himself? Where he*
          came from? What was he like?
John: *He was democratic.*
Harry: *Where did he come from? He was Cuban wasn't he?* (50)
Philip: *(Quoting from the text-book) 'He studied law at the*
          University of Havana, and became a great defender of the
          poor. . . .'
Harry: *Where did he pick up his Communist ideas?*
John: *Was he a Communist at first?* (55)
Philip: *No. He was for the people of Cuba. (Continuing to quote)*
          'He started up his movement in 1953. . . .'
Harry: *When did he overthrow Batista then?*
John: *1959. Batista fled in 1959. When Castro got in power he*
          started using his Marxist ways. This didn't please America (60)
          very much and in 1960 they cut off all relations.

Mark: *The Russians helped Cuba build up their industries and all that.*

Harry: *Yes.*

Mark: *When he became Prime Minister he started nationalizing* (65) *the industries and turning against America.*

Philip: *Yeah . . . (Quoting from text-book) 'Diplomatic relations were broken off in 1961. . . .'*

Harry: *Who was in then? Kennedy?*

John: *He came in - yeah, he came in, in 1960.* (70)

Mark: *And he supplied the Cuban revolutionaries with weapons to stage a coup on the island. In 1961. Which didn't work. They was all captured before they could do any damage.*

Harry: *Planned in the Eisenhower period was it?*

Philip: *Yeah.* (75)

Mark: *In 1960 Castro strengthened contacts with Russia and China, building up his Marxist rule.*

Harry: *Was he allied with Moscow or Peking?*

Mark: *Moscow.*

Philip: *How about the missile base?* (80)

Harry: *No. The missiles were in 1962 - we're just building up to that.*

John: *So the Bay of Pigs led to a . . . .*

Philip: *Yeah, it failed. It was a fiasco they reckon.*

Harry: *Was it condemned by people?* (85)

Mark: *It drove Cuba closer to the Communist world.*

Philip: *Russia started putting in missiles and all that.*

Harry: *So they built up links with Russia.*

John: *Then in 1962, the Cuban Missile Crisis.*

Mark: *The Russians started placing missile bases on Cuba, and* (90) *American planes, flying over Cuba, they found out. Reconnaissance planes.*

John: *Missiles were pointed at America, and they could land. . . .*

Philip: *They could land in Washington, Chicago.*

Harry: *How did Russia get their missiles out there in the first* (95) *place?*

Philip: *Ships.*

John: *Cuba's only 90 miles from the American coast.*

Harry: *What did the Americans do?*

Mark: *First, Kennedy told the Russians to take their missiles off,* (100) *which they never did. He did it diplomatically. So then he had to do something strong.*

Andrew: *Yeah, he could have had other ideas, but they'd have led to war immediately.*

John:	*So he blockaded Cuba. Ships blockade. All ships to Cuba.*	(105)
Mark:	*They had their army mobilized and 156 of their nuclear warheads.*	
John:	*Neither side wanted to back down. Kennedy would not back down. Nor would Kruschev. Things were coming to a head and one side had to make a move. If the Russians had continued putting their missiles on the island, Kennedy would have started a war. As he told them he would do.*	(110)
Harry:	*Would Kennedy have started a war, do you think?*	
Andrew:	*No, of course he wouldn't. He tried to bluff them.*	
John:	*Defence mechanism, isn't it. Got to have some. . . .*	(115)
Mark:	*Russia's a threat, isn't it. You think how close Alaska is to America.*	
Harry:	*Russia feels more threatened by the West than we do by Russia, I think.*	
Philip:	*Yeah.*	(120)
Mark:	*Russia could bomb Alaska.*	
John:	*Yeah, but there's not much on Alaska.*	
Harry:	*So Cuba - so they blocked up the shipping route.*	
Mark:	*The world was in a state of shock. A false move by either side could have caused a third world war.*	(125)
Andrew:	*Yes. But Russia offered to withdraw her weapons if N.A.T.O. offered to withdraw weapons from Turkey.*	
Harry:	*So. Turkey? N.A.T.O. wouldn't withdraw from Turkey?*	
Mark:	*No. Missiles were removed from Turkey.*	
Harry:	*They did?*	(130)
Mark:	*Yeah, but Russia didn't back down. Kennedy had to. . . .*	
John:	*They didn't keep to their side of the bargain.*	
Philip:	*No.*	
Mark:	*They did in the end.*	
John:	*Yeah. Under United Nations supervision they did. This helped America to lift the blockade.*	(135)
Mark:	*An arrangement was set upon that no weapons would be placed - if Russia never placed missiles on Cuba the Americans would leave Cuba alone. They wouldn't impose any sanctions on the island.*	(140)
John:	*October 62.*	
Harry:	*How long did the crisis last?*	
John:	*Two weeks.*	
Harry:	*What's happened since 1962?*	
John:	*Well Cuba's a Communist country but it's got no real backing.*	(145)
Andrew:	*It's like Yugoslavia.*	

Harry:	Well not really.
John:	He's Russian, but he doesn't want to be led by Russia.
Andrew:	Not aligned with Moscow. Not aligned with America, a (150) non-aligned country. Recently head of the Conference of non-aligned countries.
Mark:	In the Cuban crisis they set up a hot-line between Washington and Moscow.
Harry:	Really? (155)
John:	Yeah. And this upset China.
Harry:	What upset Castro?
John:	Hot-line between Washington and Moscow after the crisis.
Mark:	That, and the test-ban treaty, was one of the results of the Cuban crisis. (160)
John:	In 1963 the U.S. agreed it would never make any more test explosions. China sneered at Kruschev. Reckoned Russia was lily-livered because backing down. And called America a paper tiger.
Harry:	Has there been any American incidents in Cuba since (165) 1962?
Philip:	No.
Harry:	What's Cuba done since?
John:	They're a small state with no real power. They're there. They're like a thorn in the side of. . . . (170)
Mark:	They're more like a symbol of defiance really.
John:	The terrorists go there.
Andrew:	You can't say they have no real power. They nearly caused a world war.
John:	It wasn't them. It was the Russians. (175)
Andrew:	They have got power. They can try - revolutions - South America, like Bolivia. Was it Bolivia?
John:	But since 1962 they haven't done all that much.
Andrew:	But in South America and South Africa they have. Angola. (180)
Harry:	So, America has the threat of a small state who won't do as they're told right on their shores nearly.
John:	He - Castro - confiscated all the American property on the island.
Harry:	Is that the reason for the Bay of Pigs then? (185)
Mark:	Another thing that should be mentioned is the way the Americans staged mock invasions of the island.
John:	And Norway.
Mark:	As if they were getting ready for the War.
Harry:	So what have we got then, so far? (190)

John:	*Intro about the Spanish-American War. Then American influence post the first world war.*
Philip:	*Then Batista and him being overthrown by Castro.*
Harry:	*And the bit about Castro's background.*
John:	*They - the Bay of Pigs. Then the Missiles Crisis.* (195)
Harry:	*And the final paragraph about recent times.*
John:	*Yeah.*
Philip:	*Yeah.*
Harry:	*That's about it, then.*
Mark:	*You could put something in about the way both the* (200) *countries saw it as a whim - in the Cold War.*
Andrew:	*A whim? The Russians saw it as a whim?*
John:	*Well. . . .*
Mark:	*They might have momentarily gained victory.*
Andrew:	*They've gained Cuba.* (205)
Harry:	*Have they, though?*
John:	*It leans more towards Russia than it does towards America.*
Harry:	*What if Castro was to suddenly die? What would happen then?* (210)
Philip:	*I don't think anybody knows.*
John:	*Same thing with Tito. Nobody knows.*
Harry:	*But Tito's just died!*
Andrew:	*He could always be assassinated.*
Harry:	*Who'd assassinate him - the Americans?* (215)
John:	*No. It'd cause them too much trouble.*
Andrew:	*No one could prove anything.*
Harry:	*Did Castro go to America?*
John:	*Yeah. He talked to the U.N.*
Harry:	*Did he? Would he be the spokesman of the non-aligned* (220) *countries?*
Philip:	*What's non-aligned?*
Harry:	*Well, not on the Russian side, not on the American side.*
Philip:	*What about Britain? Is that non-aligned?*
Harry:	*No.* (225)
Others:	*No.*
Philip:	*That's about it, then.*

What Are the Underlying Features of This Discussion?

There seem to us to be four distinct but interrelated factors at work here. These are:

   1. The particular ways in which the participants *work* together, or in other words, the kinds of conventions they observe in their working;

2. The ways in which they *think* about their task, the qualities of their thinking;
3. The *knowledge* on which they draw as they go about the task and finally;
4. The kind of language they use.

We will now look at the discussion with reference to each of these in turn.

The Ways In Which They Work Together
Of all the various features that characterize the work of the group there is one that is most striking, so it seems appropriate to begin there.

The Emergence of a Dominating Member of the Group
The dominating member is of course Harry. He emerges rapidly, and not only does he establish the strategy or plan of campaign by which to handle the task in front of them, but he also creates the procedures which will allow everyone to contribute. He could do this in the way conversationalists often operate, by literally asking X or Y what they think. Instead of doing this, he opts for the technique of eliciting information from others which he himself, fairly obviously, could have presented. He discreetly feigns ignorance, and poses questions for the others to answer, as if he does not himself know the answers. For example:

Harry: Did they support Castro?
John: Yeah, they encouraged a resistance movement?
Harry: In the 50s?
John: Drawing to the 60s. (line 25)

His own command of the broad area of the subject is revealed whenever he checks others from overlooking key facts or misrepresenting them, but even then he prefers the method of presenting information in question form, for the others to check and examine. Thus he asks, of the Bay of Pigs incident:

Planned in the Eisenhower period was it? (line 74)

and continues later to pursue the idea that Kennedy's policy was, in part at least, the product of earlier decisions by other politicians. His dominance, and the same technique of leadership in the guise of open questions, persist to the end of the discussion. It is he who asks the marvellous question, line 210,

What if Castro was to suddenly die? What would happen then?

And a little later, line 218:

Did Castro go to America? . . . Would he be the spokesman of the non-aligned countries?

But it must be noted that his dominance is not totalitarian. He does not say significantly more than others, nor does he intimidate others. Nor does he command the more taciturn members of the group to speak up and speak out. It is perhaps for this reason that his dominance works and persists.

Acceptance of Each Other's Contributions

They are extremely good at accepting the various points made by each other. Without ever having to say so in so many words, they repeatedly demonstrate that they are working well together. This allows the discussion to thrive, but it also in some ways inhibits the participants from following through some of the possibilities, on a semantic dimension, inherent in what they are saying and doing. (This is bound to be, as we point out later.) It is a solidarity which manifests itself in two main ways. First, there is a large amount of *agreement* that is based more on the need for agreement than on agreement with what is being said. In some discussions there are long stretches of dialogue at the beginning where the participants simply repeat each other's contributions in their own words, perhaps adding an illustration or anecdote to embellish it, and then pausing to wait for somebody else to follow suit. On this occasion there is no such repetition, but there is a fair amount of tacit agreement where, perhaps, there should be disagreement. In effect, it is a way of holding a group together by not exposing any member of it to criticism or correction. Thus when Harry is told that Eisenhower and Truman were both Democrats, he replies:

I thought Eisenhower was Republican. I'm not sure. I'm not sure. (line 36)

And thus allows John to pursue the facts for himself:

I'll look it up.

Deliberate Role-play

Related to this determination to accept what the group has to offer, is a willingness to play one's part accordingly. A discussion, like any other social activity, is a game in which all the participants play their respective parts. Harry plays his particular part, throwing out questions to which he knows the answers, keeping the discussion on a fairly narrow and specific line, but he is only able to do this because the others both allow him to and help him to. Philip accepts his requirement that they delay the topic of the Castro revolution (line 11). John and later Mark repeatedly present fully coherent answers to Harry's many questions. Andrew allows more than one excellent contribution to be dropped in the interests of group cohesion, and allows Harry to leave his excellent point about Angola (line 179) in order to keep to Harry's general sense of where their discussion is going. In this way, it could be realistically argued that all five participants are equally dominant, in that none of them is pushed out or kept down by the others, nor seeking to push them out or keep them down. It is in fact a highly democratic discussion, and it is worth stressing that this is so despite the fact that, in terms of quantity or size of contributions, the different participants are not equal. It seems that this kind of inequality is a basic feature of a good discussion, and can only be avoided by the introduction of a highly formal and rehearsed ritual, as with parliamentary procedure. But there is a great deal of loss in such procedure, and very little gain.

This deliberate role-play is also shown in the talkers' *willingness to take turns* in the discussion, such that everyone contributes in some measure at some stage. Mark does not actually speak up until fairly late, - about line 62 - and Andrew does not speak until much later still - line 103. But both of them make very valuable contributions which indicate they have been fully involved from the start. What is important is that nobody is stopped from contributing, and the dominance of one member does not inhibit the contributions of others. It is a tacit part of the proceedings that everyone can speak up, but that they will do so in turn. Nobody is shouted down, and nobody is simply ignored.

Statements as Questions

Also, on a fair number of occasions, *statements are made in the form of questions,* and of open-ended questions specifically. Some of the questions are rhetorical: 'Shall we put in a bit about Castro himself?' (line 47) clearly means that we shall put in a bit about Castro himself. But elsewhere the questions are 'genuine' - as with Harry's, 'Where did he pick up his communist ideas?' (line 54) which, in fact, is never answered. A similar technique, as noted already, is the presenting of questions to elicit information which the questioner already possesses - much as a teacher regularly does in the classroom. But unlike many teachers, the questioner here does not generally make it clear that he knows what he wants the others to tell him. Indeed the use of questions in this fashion is complementary to the generally tentative, as opposed to dogmatic, style in which a great deal (but not all) of the conversation is couched. Thus Harry concludes his correction about the presidents of the U.S.A., with the comment, 'I'm not sure' (line 36) and concludes one of his major (and most interesting) assertions, 'Russia feels more threatened by the West than we do by Russia' (line 118) with the rider - 'I think.'

Detachment and Impersonality

Finally, despite a fairly direct and spontaneous (and sustained) conversation, they remain quite *impersonal and detached;* no one sulks, no one demoralizes any one else, no one walks out or opts out. This allows Philip, for instance, in the closing moments of the discussion, to ask a quite basic question which elsewhere he might well have been made to feel foolish for having (or daring) to ask: 'What about Britain? Is that non-aligned?' (line 224).

These, then, are some of the methods by which the group set to work, or to use the term which we prefer, these are some of the *conventions.* There is thus a substantial formality in the midst of an apparent informality. The group have employed no titles for each other, such as 'Mr President' or 'Mr Chairman'. Nor have they used points of order and points of information. They do not even use each other's names. Yet they are deeply formal for all that, observing conventions which they could not themselves necessarily identify.

Conventions They Do Not Employ

There are also certain conventions which they do *not* employ and which might possibly have proved useful. For example, nobody ever says, 'That's very interesting, could you go back on that?' or words to that effect. There is, for that reason, very little *back-pedalling,* and some excellent 'asides' are left behind, unutilized. Thus Mark's statement that Russia could bomb Alaska (line 121) and Andrew's statement that Cuba's condition is not unlike that of Yugoslavia (line 147) are both discarded prematurely. Both contain the germ of very fruitful lines of thinking. Additionally, they do not find a fruitful convention for *handling their text-book.* The two or three occasions when they use it, they do not pursue it very thoroughly. They do not, as it were, say, 'Maybe the text-book will tell us something different from that, or will disagree with what we have just said.' They use the book for agreement rather than for provocation. And on the various occasions when they are in clear doubt as to the precise facts of the matter, they do not use the book to clarify what the facts are. They begin to do so (line 50) when they are clarifying basic points about Castro's personal background, but even here they do not push very hard or very far. They need someone to suggest that they establish some of the various facts together, and then check them from the book. Better still, they need to pursue their sources on a wider canvas in the school library. Similarly, they do not do something which would have helped them to keep tabs on the points they make and to wander off in pursuit of new details and new ideas without losing their main thread: they do not take *any kind of written note.* If, for example, they had been urged from the start to jot down any interesting points emerging in the discussion, and which are not necessarily resolved in the discussion itself, they would have been left, at the end, with a number of fruitful questions for later discussion which otherwise are lost and forgotten. Of course, learning to spot these valuable 'asides' is an art unto itself.

The Ways in Which They Think About Their Task

A number of features characterize the ways in which they think about what they are doing.

Establishing a Strategy

The group quickly establish an overall strategy around which to organize their thinking. They decide not only to plan the essay along chronological lines (which the essay title demands they do) but also to conduct the discussion in this way also. The interesting thing is that not only could they have operated differently, but that the drift of their actual conversation is itself different. They keep on becoming absorbed in ideas that cut across the strict chronology of their thinking and which lead them back to ideas that they have left behind. Moreover, they do not know enough about some of the material (such as Batista) to fully utilize it in any chronological sense.

They not only establish their strategy, they constantly insist on keeping to it. It dominates everything they do. Harry very early on stops Philip from leaping down the time-scale from The Spanish-American War to Castro's revolution (line 12) and continues to insist on a proper sense of time and sequence throughout the discussion. So too, he twice asks that they explore the question of what has happened since 1962 (lines 144 and 168). Likewise, he stops Philip from galloping through the time-sequence from 1960 to 1962:

> No. The missiles were in 1962 - we're just building up to that. (line 81)

In this way, they almost deliberately fail to explore areas of their own knowledge and experience which might have helped them considerably in their task - a point we will return to shortly.

Coming to a Conclusion and Adding the Postscript

Central to the idea of establishing and adhering to a strategy, is the achieving of that strategy and hence of drawing things to a close and coming to your conclusion. And this usually involves some kind of recapitulation of what has been said.

Thus Harry says (line 190), 'So what have we got then, so far?' and John then proceeds to spell out the shape of their essay, beginning with the introductory paragraph. They then move very rapidly through the rest of their essay, leading Harry to remark, only ten lines later (line 199) - 'That's about it, then.' But, of course, that is not it at all, for after the summing-up comes *the postscript.* Some of the best moments in any discussion come when people agree that the bulk of their work is finished, perhaps because this is when the basic strategy they have used for their discussion can be relaxed, and when those points which in effect the strategy has not permitted to be made, can, at last, be made. On this occasion, Harry's optimistic assertion - 'That's about it, then' is immediately followed by a totally new idea from Mark (line 200), 'You could put something in about the way both the countries saw it as a whim. . . .' This, in turn, leads to another quite different rider from Harry, 'What if Castro was to suddenly die?' which, in turn, leads to the idea of his possibly being assassinated, which is raised by Andrew (line 214). In many ways this short final section of the discussion is more rich in possibilities than all of the rest of it, but these possibilities are raised only lightly, and are left hanging in the air - as is the way with a postscript.

The Strategy: Its Disadvantages

No strategy is perfect. Every strategy carries within itself certain limitations. It becomes an inhibiting factor, just as it also becomes an enabling factor. You cannot do without some such strategy, and there are certain things you cannot do with it. One of the ways in which they are held back by their strategy in this case, is that they become so absorbed in the business of sequence and chronology that they often think they have thought something out when all they have done is to place it in chronological order. Thus, they offer no real explanation for the rise and fall of Batista apart from John's statement, in line 19, that - 'during the 50s he became a tyrant to his country so the Americans cut off their supplies.' There is no exploration of the reasons for America's initial support, nor of what went wrong. The fact that sequence is their main concern means also that they do not at any point define any of the main terms they employ, and there is, therefore, a great deal of imprecision running right through the discussion, or (to be more precise!) a great deal of vagueness. The concepts - Communist, Marxist, Republican, Democrat and democratic are employed without any definitions being offered. They seem to take it for granted that they know roughly what these words mean, and leave it at that. Harry's diplomatic suggestion that Eisenhower was of a different political persuasion from his predecessor seems to imply that he thinks there is a significance in this fact, but he does not pursue the point. As a consequence a great deal of what is incomplete, such as Castro's initial appeal in the eyes of America and his later antagonism towards the American system and his rejection by the American government, is in no way explained. The nearest they get to doing so, is Mark's statement (line 65) - 'When he became Prime Minister he started nationalizing the industries and turning against America', but they do not pursue this point. Nobody asks what he did do that in any way offended the

Americans. They come very near indeed though, to asking this when John says (line 183), 'He - Castro - confiscated all the American property on the island' to which Harry then asks, 'It that the reason for the Bay of Pigs then?' But again, the point is not pursued.

In fact their strategy is weakened throughout by their failure to spend time introducing and establishing it. They plunge into it without really *orientating* themselves. This is an aspect of the work to which we return more fully in relation to discursive writing in the final chapters.

The Strategy: Its Advantages

But if the participants' own sense of purpose and method to some extent blinds them to important possibilities, it also helps them to *contribute and to learn* a great deal. A vast amount of thinking is apparent, not only in the juxtaposing of a large amount of factual material (itself, no mean achievement) but also in the ways in which many areas of uncertainty are probed and interesting questions raised. For instance, the lines following Harry's question - 'What's Cuba done since?' (line 168) contain a rich sequence of fascinating and relevant points, each one of which could provide a whole session unto itself. John's assertion that Cuba has no 'real power' leads to Mark's comment that it is 'a symbol of defiance'. John's sequel to this almost contradicts what he has just said: 'The terrorists go there'. However, he does not explain what this actually means. It does, however, prompt Andrew to dispute the idea that the Cubans have no real power and to justify his point, briefly but cogently.

At the same time, some of the most penetrating and most creative ideas are raised and then lost all too quickly. Mark's suggestion that the Russians did not, at first, see what they were doing as profoundly significant (line 200); Andrew's suggestion that the Russians have 'gained' Cuba (line 205) and his earlier comparison between Cuba and Yugoslavia (line 147); and Harry's question, 'What if Castro was to suddenly die' (line 209); and Andrew's suggestion that he could be assassinated (line 214) - all these are, as it were, pearls that are left behind. In other words, *the discussion is not the last word.* It is only a stage in a sequence, leaving points to be extrapolated and developed later. It is only one lesson, one session, in a great series.

In this respect, though, a discussion is no different from any other learning activity. Much is achieved, and much is indicated for what is to follow. No matter how formalized the activity, this is bound to be the case. Centuries of thought (and development) have gone into the procedures of a criminal court, but cases are still taken on appeal to 'higher' courts, and even when the appeal procedures have been exhausted, mistakes are still made. There is still more to be said, books to be written about the mistakes, and even, occasionally, mistakes to be acknowledged. Similarly, nothing that has ever been thought out is incapable of rethinking. Indeed, it could be fairly claimed that the best thinking is that which throws up the greatest number of invitations or stimuli for rethinking, for beginning again. Note also that the best ideas in this discussion come later, rather than earlier. Perhaps this is because the earlier parts of any such occasion are in effect devoted to getting the project off the ground, such that the need for social solidarity becomes the sub-text, as it were, of what is being said. Once this has been established, much more disagreement can be tolerated, and hence much more creativity. Sometimes this means that the contributors who are most critical remain quiet for the main part of the proceedings. In this instance, Andrew, who is the least easily satisfied of the group, does not say anything at all until over half-way through the proceedings. Note also that most of the best moments in the discussion emanate from questions rather than statements. Obviously there needs to be a substantial balance between the two, but it is the questioners who push the boat out (and rock the boat) rather than the respondents, as with Andrew's, 'A whim?' (line 202) and Harry's, 'Have they though?' (line 206).

The Inequality of Effort

Another feature of their thinking is the inequality of effort on the part of the various participants. The extent to which they actually seek to think on their feet, to utilize what they know, in order to fulfil the task in front of them, is itself unequal among the different members of the group. It is an obvious point to make, it follows logically from the behaviour of all the group (and not just one or two of them) and it is an important point to make, because it directly affects the role of the teacher. On this occasion, it is Philip who is the least engaged in thinking about the subject. All his contributions tend to bring the subject to a close, rather than enrich the group's understanding of it. His leap from one end of the time-scale to the other, at the very beginning of the discussion, is typical of his later contributions. His finest moment is at the very end, when he actually asks the meaning of something he does not understand - 'What's non-aligned?' (line 222), but even then he soon accepts a brief answer and again brings the proceedings to a close. Similarly, a little earlier, he gives the most facile answer - 'I don't think anybody knows' (line 211) to the excellent question about Castro's possible death and the sequel to that death. Obviously the extent of such inequality will vary from one discussion to another, but it is a feature of discussions of all kinds. One alternative is to impose some conventional structure where everyone has to contribute in very specific ways, as in the very ritualized discussions of a parliament, law court or debate. But these demand a professionalism, a command of the subject as well as of the method of discussion, which are contrary to what the classroom is seeking to do, for such proceedings are committed, not so much to learning, as to display (of both subject and method). Other means, though, are available to the teacher in seeking to overcome this inequality, and we will come to these later. But it is important to note that while Philip is the one member of the group who does not add very much, if anything, to anybody else's thinking and understanding, he does nevertheless play his part. He offers some suggestions. He refers to the text-book. He accepts the direction of others. He plays the game. If he had not done this, there would have been no discussion or it would have finished very quickly.

The Knowledge on Which They Draw

All discussion, like all forms of thinking, is rooted in various kinds of knowledge of the topic to hand. Some of this knowledge is used; some of it is taken for granted, treated as not needing to be said; and some of it is dismissed as irrelevant.

The Assumptions They Make

There are many things which they know, but which they assume that everyone else knows, and hence do not have to be spelt out. For example, they do not actually clarify the precise identity of Castro for the benefit of someone who does not know about him, or, more appropriately, for the benefit of providing suitable background information for the essay. Similarly, they do not locate Cuba geographically any more than they locate other places such as Alaska, or Bolivia, or the U.S.A.

In a different way, they take it for granted that Castro is synonymous with Cuba, Kruschev with Russia and Kennedy with the U.S.A. This is not to imply that they are at fault in doing so. To the contrary, some such assumptions have to be made or they would be for ever stopping to define and explain. The significant thing is that some of these assumptions, while entirely rational in themselves, have consequences which weaken the discussion. For example, the geographical relationship of Cuba to the U.S.A., which they mention only very briefly at one point, is absolutely central to the whole issue of United States' involvement in Cuban history. The same applies to the geographical-economic factors of Cuba's natural resources. These two phenomena, the geographical relationship and the geographical-economic background, provide two basic answers to America's political and economic involvement in Cuba, but these are not touched on in the discussion. As a result, most of the events they talk about are to a large extent unmotivated, even though they venture to spell out some sort of motivation from time to time, as with the suggestion that Batista became a tyrant and this led to the withdrawal of American support. They are on firmer ground, of course, with the whole business of the missile base, where the motivation for the actions of both sides is more explicit and clear.

Gaps and Errors

The discussion reveals a number of important gaps in their knowledge. They seem to know little about Batista, for instance, and the fact that they say so little about recent events in Angola or Cuba's encouragement to South American revolutionaries suggests that they know fairly little about them. There are also some simple errors, as when the terms Democrat and democratic are confused.

Relevance and Irrelevance

More important than any such errors is that they leave out of the discussion whole areas of knowledge that are familiar to them, and which might well enrich their thinking. They base these decisions (explicitly or implicitly) on their sense of what is and what is not *relevant* to the task they are engaged in. In many discussions somebody is checked by the cry - 'But that's off the point!' or, 'What's that got to do with it?' On this occasion the group employ more subtle equivalents, as when Harry comments, 'Wait a minute' in order to stop Philip breaking the chain of his strategy (line 12), and later employs the simple tactic of changing the subject in order to escape from what he sees as various dead-ends. Thus he leaves the topic of a possible Russian attack on Alaska by the emphatic statement: 'So Cuba - so they blocked up the shipping route' (line 123), again bringing the discussion back to the initial conception. On the other hand, several major points are introduced which are allowed to pass the test of relevance and which quite possibly might have failed to do so. Thus, Mark's mention of the hot-line between Moscow and Washington (line 153) is assimilated into the discussion, as is the brief exploration of the earlier career of Castro (line 47). But another interesting suggestion by Mark that they should mention America's more recent staging of a mock invasion (line 186) seems to be excluded by Harry's comment, 'So what have we got then, so far?' (line 190).

Their sense of what is relevant is based not simply in the particular strategy they have adopted, but more fundamentally in their sense of what history is all about. They have a fairly narrow view of what history consists of. Specifically, it is public events presented in some sort of chronological sequence. These events are not seen naïvely. There is a definite awareness of the complexity of motivations that drive nations on collision courses. Thus, the missile crisis is portrayed as a delicate state of affairs where 'a false move by either side' could have upset the apple cart, and which, in its turn, gives rise to a complicated sequence of counter-moves by the opposing sides. Even so, history is seen as primarily a list of events arranged chronologically and, as we have seen earlier, this is the strategy around which the whole discussion revolves.

But of course the essay title itself is equally influential. It asks for a sequence of events, and they therefore construct their talking around the idea of just such a sequence. In fact, though, other strategies would also be viable for the discussion itself. They could begin by noting the main sequential facts and then digress to elaborate on the most important of these. This might mean some such pattern as: Batista - his rise and fall; Castro - early American attitudes towards and personal background; the missile crisis; recent events including Angola. One of the difficulties with a purely chronological approach to history is that each event in its turn leads backwards and forwards across the time-span, such that the 'and then . . .' approach becomes unworkable, as it threatens to do here.

So we could say that the group are weakened in the vigour and originality of their thinking by their very natural (and indeed proper!) sense of *what is relevant to history,* and *what is relevant to discussion* leading to the planning of a history essay. In effect, what would help them on a subsequent occasion would be a more liberal view of the process of discussion itself. Ideally, they need to see discussion as something presenting opportunities of its own, as something viable and valuable unto itself. For example, they do not utilize any personal or subjective knowledge, even though they are dealing with people individually when speaking of Castro, Kennedy and Kruschev, and collectively, when referring to American, the Russian and the Cuban peoples. As a result there is no real sense of people being involved at all. Even when the world holds its breath in the missile crisis, it remains a very impersonal world. The nearest they get to penetrating this, is the brief allusion to Russian fear of the West in contrast to Western fears of Russia, but this is not pursued at all. It is history, in other words, without personal involvement, without relationship to personal experience, without and hypothesizing as to why people, in general or in particular, behave as they do. More precisely, the hypotheses do not go beyond agreed public facts. It is history without very much psychology. It is also history without very much geography or economics - both subjects which this particular group are studying. And it is history without sociology. Interestingly, the group were at this time studying Karl Marx.

These comments are not criticisms of this particular task or of this group of students. They do not invalidate the task. To the contrary, it is a useful part of the process of learning and offers a number of important possibilities for the teacher to pursue later.

The Language They Use

Linguists have long ago pointed out that there is the language of verse, and the language of prose, and then there is the spoken language. Throughout their school careers, pupils are asked to read prose and also to write it, but this is not what they speak. First, conversation does not arrange itself into sentences. Indeed a great deal of conversation resists conventional punctuation. The tone of voice, its pitch and rhythm, in various ways replaces punctuation, as do a whole variety of paralinguistic factors such as gesture, movement and facial expression. Equally important is the emotional-social experience itself, for as people get carried away with what is being said, so they carry others with them.

The Spoken Language

The discussion on this occasion contains a number of half-finished thoughts, such as John's (line 13 - 'Something about 1900 to 1930s. . . .' And John also says later (line 41 - 'He started up his group in the highlands or whatever it was.' Similarly, Philip says (line 87 - 'Russia started putting in missiles and all that.' None of these usages of the language would be acceptable in most forms of prose.

Similarly, there are a number of linguistic *errors* - a concept which we wish to explore later, in the next chapter. John says at line 25, for example, 'Drawing to the 60s . . .' when he probably should have said, 'Coming down to. . . .'

It is also worth adding that the transcript we have made here of this particular group discussion is not only a representation of what was said, but also a *misrepresentation.* Conversation resists a literal transcription. People's contributions overlap, and parts of some of them are lost, inaudible. Moreover, everything that is said has a pitch, tone and rhythm, and there is no accessible way of recapturing these. Even if one scores a conversation, as some linguists do, as if it were a quintet or a symphony, the real meaning (which is itself partly dramatic) is still elusive.

Register

Likewise, the *register* of discursive talk is to some extent distinct from other spoken registers. What do we mean by *register?* We use register to refer to the particular type of language that is accepted as appropriate to particular purposes. Thus, one can talk of the register of a formal interview, of a newspaper report, of a friendly chat, and so on. In a literal sense, there are millions and millions of different registers for no two chats are ever quite the same, nor are two newspaper reports. But for practical everyday purposes, everyone has a rough sense of the register that is appropriate for a given occasion, and very often people have a very exact sense of what is appropriate.

Register is the broad term covering the use of language for any particular purpose. Each register is identified by its *conventions,* by those attributes which distinguish the language of, say, a parliamentary debate from a cross-examination in a law court. Such conventions may take numerous forms such as, who speaks to whom, and when, and for how long, and using what mode of address. They occur, of course, in writing as well as in all kinds of talking, and they are linked also to non-linguistic conventions such as ways of dressing.

Understanding the language used on any occasion is in part a matter of understanding the register and its attendant conventions. Understanding a parliamentary debate, for example, whether as observer or would-be participant, is partly a matter of internalizing the various conventions which govern the course of the debate. In a very different way, a child watching a movie has in some sense to understand the conventions of the film-maker, to come to terms with devices such as the flashback, cut, dissolve, and 'meanwhile, back on the farm. . . .'

Similarly, the child has to become familiar with the conventions of, say, an examination essay in history and to distinguish these from the conventions of reporting an experiment in chemistry. These various conventions pertain not only to the kinds of language to be employed, but also to the layout of the work, the use of headings and sub-headings and abbreviations, and also to the use of illustrations. The learner has to be familiar with these various registers in order to understand them when seeking to read and interpret them, and also in order to create them for himself or herself. The teacher's task is to ensure that the learner comes to distinguish the various conventions of each register, and especially to meet plenty of models of each register in use. In this particular discussion, the participants' language is characterized, as we have noted earlier, by an *impersonal* tone, or, in effect, by an absence of drama. Indeed, it is so impersonal that no names are employed at any stage of the discussion. Also, the various assertions and statements are constantly related to *questions* and then to further questions. There are virtually no rhetorical questions.

In addition, the discussion displays aspects of virtually all kinds of talking: the incomplete units of language, the occasional errors, the liberal scattering of overlapping contributions, of interruptions and vocal 'fill-ins', of 'ums' and 'ahs' and 'yeahs'. In other words, the language of discussion is not the language of discursive written prose. And this has two corollaries.

First, the mere fact that discussion takes place does not itself mean that everyone can then write a discursive essay. Discursive essays are not simply discussions written down. There is a vast linguistic gap between the two. And secondly, the value of a discussion does not lie simply in the quality (or lack of it) of the written work that follows it.

Summary

We have suggested that four factors are at work in this particular group discussion and that each one radically affects the quality of the discussion as a whole:

1. The particular ways in which the participants work together;

2. The ways in which they think about their task;

3. The knowledge on which they draw;

4. The language they use.

In the next chapter we look at these four factors in more detail, so that we can later use them in looking at what happens not only in talking but also in reading and in writing.

In the following chapter (Chapter 3) we return to the business of discussion, looking at some of the differences between group discussion and class discussion, and at the teacher's role in both.

2
Getting It Right

Introduction

Teachers and pupils alike are endlessly concerned with 'getting it right'. This chapter looks at some of the ways in which things can go wrong, so that teachers can help to put them right. We outline something like a dozen problems which can bedevil the learner at any point of the curriculum. Learning difficulties can emanate from any one of them or from any combination of them.

The Knowledge on Which We Draw

On any given occasion we employ only a tiny fraction of what we already know. Our decisions as to what to employ and what not to employ, are based on a number of *tacit assumptions* from which various difficulties can follow.

The Problem of Relevance

In the discussion on Cuban history which we looked at in Chapter 1, the participants impose a strict sense of what is and what is not relevant to their task, but still manage to sustain a quite fruitful and lively discussion. More common is the situation where pupils are fatally inhibited by a sense that nothing they know is relevant to the task in front of them. Take for example, the following piece of writing by a 16-year-old girl, produced as part of a course in Child Care. One of her assignments has been to 'adopt' a small child living in her neighbourhood and to record the child's development in the form of a diary. Here are some extracts from Marina's record of Paul's development through the two years of the course.

MARINA'S DIARY

Date: 14.9.78.
Paul - Age 23 months
Today when I took Paul out I noticed a lot of different, first of all I saw him sitting on the toilet. His mum told me he only had a nappy on

*at night. When Paul's mum put his shoes on Paul undid the buckle
and took them off again. When we we already to go we said goodbye
and I walked to the library and inside Paul was running about a lot, so
I had to carry him. Paul looked at some books and was very interested
in them and tried to say some words. When we got home, he had a
glass of orange then I took him home.*

Date: 1.12.78.
Age 2 yrs 2 mths
*Paul is still 2 stone and talking more each day so you have to be very
careful what you say because he copies you. Today I learnt Paul to hit
a ball with a bat and we played a kind of cricket.*

Date: 9.1.79.
Age 2 yrs 3 mths
*Paul has learnt a new word he can now say water but in 2 different
parts like wa - er. Tonight I washed Paul and all the time he was gig-
gles and kept saying water.*

Date: 20.3.79.
Age 2 yrs 5 mths
*Yesterday I came home from America, when I first saw Paul I was
really surprised because (i) he looked fatter in the face: (ii) he is speaking a lot more: (iii) he reckoned me straight away: (iiii) he dose'nt wear
a nappy anymore. When he saw me he said Rina. I brought Paul a cup
with mickey mouse on and a teashirt with mickey on, and a pair of
shorts. So every time I go round there he gets his cup and comes running towards me saying rina, and he keeps kissing me saying ta rina.*

Final entry
Date 20.4.80.
Age 3 yrs 6 mths
*I am now coming to the last of my diaries and as you will notice Paul
has changed a great deal and has developed his own little character
and personality. I have enjoyed every minute moment of being with
him and I shall see him quite often still. Paul is quite a nice boy and
quite pleasant but he still has little odd moment like every other boy. I
think he will grow up to be a very placid and carefree man, I think he
is wonderful.*

Although the writing has many nice touches, and shows a warm enjoy-
ment of the experience of meeting and getting to know the small child, there
are major areas of possible exploration that Marina does not touch upon, or
which are touched upon very briefly. There is no venture into Paul's own
growing awareness of himself, of what Paul appears to think or feel or

mean. His language development is briskly mentioned - 'He is speaking a lot more' - but there is no mapping out of the particular ways and means by which this development occurs, no reference to other children, no reference to what her own mother can tell her about her own development by way of comparison. In this way, Marina is not only failing to explore new territory, but is also failing to explore territory that is partly familiar to herself. She is making few links with the rest of her experience, and this might well be the next step for the teacher to help her towards. In effect, she needs *to extend the map* within which she explores the topic of the child's development.

It must be stressed that a sense of relevance is a part of all projects. To direct one's thinking towards some kind of end or target, is to sort out (and reject most of) what we already know. Thus learning something new - a topic or an entire 'subject' - means not just learning what goes into it, but also what is to be left out. Sometimes this is a fairly simple matter, or at least seems to be so. History is not geography; economics is not physics. But, of course, things may not be quite so simple. In many important historical issues a knowledge of geography is essential, for example. And in the development of the curricula of schools, there are now massive overlaps from one subject to the next. Moral education, religion, social studies, history, health education, literature and language - all are tied up with each other, are concerned with each other's subject-matter even though each may be presented as in some measure autonomous.

Children coming new to a subject very quickly pick up the underlying theme of what is and what is not relevant. As a consequence they quite often push out of their minds more or less everything they know. In fact, such a process makes it very difficult indeed for them to learn. In particular, such a process (sometimes aided and abetted by teachers) confuses the experience of learning with the finished and formalized body of knowledge involved. It confuses, for example, the ways in which we come to understand how the Second World War came about and what it was, with the writings of professional historians on such a subject. The latter may say nothing at all about Uncle George who fought in the War, or may not take us down the street where the bomb fell in 1942, and it may not adopt any kind of personal voice whatsoever. But all such experiences play their part in the growth of our understanding.

In effect, keeping an open mind on the question of what is and what is not relevant is an important part of learning. But students often close their own access to whole areas of what they know, because they decide too quickly that they are irrelevant.

The Problem of Values

Underlying all activity is a second kind of assumption which has to do with our values and moral attitudes. In part, our values are those things we know so well that we take them for granted and do not need to spell them out. The problem at certain times is that these underlying attitudes need to be spelt out before our thinking can in any way change or develop.

Two Children and Their Stories: The Underlying Values

One basic way of changing people's values is by getting them to be aware of and to spell out what they believe, such that they can change their position. Education is very much involved in this activity, with, of course, greatly varying degrees of success and failure. A basic difficulty for any teacher is knowing not only *how* to develop greater self-awareness but also *when*. The popular tendency is to assert that when is now - in other words, to insist that every opportunity should be taken to encourage people to rethink their values, usually by being 'corrected' and 'told'. Whether this is a fruitful policy is another matter.

For example's sake, compare the underlying values embodied in these two pieces of work. The first is an anecdote, told by a 12-year-old boy to his English teacher, in a relaxed and friendly atmosphere:

> *One day, me and George Barrymore, we made a Guy and we went out guying and we made a lot of money. We went into C & A and this boy stopped us. His name was Robert Samperson. And I said, 'What do you want?' - 'Nothing!' And I said, 'Get out of the way.' And he did not move. So I pulled out the knife and ran at him with it. And I cut his arm a bit. Then I dropped the knife and when I went to pick it up he jumped on my back and he beat me up. George Barrymore put me in the pram and took me home. And my Mum said, 'Who done that?' And I said, 'Robert Samperson!' And so my Mum cleaned me up and she went round in the car. And we got out of the car because we saw him. And my Mum goes to him, 'Come here!' He goes, 'Why?' And he comes to my Mum, 'What do you want?' And my Mum goes, 'Do you see what you done to him?' And he goes, 'I know!' And he said that I pulled a knife at him. And I said, 'That's right. Because he tried to steal my money.' And he walked away, and my Mum goes, 'Come here!' And he goes, 'Why?' And he said something. And my Mum said, 'What?' And he goes, 'You silly deaf cow!' So me and my brother ran after him. I twisted his arm up to his neck and took him to my Mum. And we took him round to his house to tell his Mum what he had done. And she said, 'Good!' And we walked away and she said, 'We will call the police to you!' And I said, 'Good riddance to you!'*

The boy telling the story makes a number of assumptions of a radical kind (as, of course, must all story-tellers!). He does not query the instantaneous decision to pull out the knife. He who hesitates is lost! Nor does he pause for the possibility that his opponent's assault on himself is in any way the fair consequence of his own assault on the opponent. Nor does he question the supportive role of his mother. Mothers are not here to examine moral problems but to act in defence of their injured sons. Hence the visit to the enemy's Mother has an almost ritualistic quality. Nothing would have been more surprising to any of the parties than her going over to the other side and not visiting vengeance on the enemy.

The anecdote recounts a moral crisis and is full of potential disaster - the knife, the battle of the Mums - without at any point indicating a change in attitudes, a questioning of values. This is not to say it necessarily should indicate any such thing, but merely to illustrate the teacher's dilemma. Should the assumptions be questioned? The anecdote also illustrates in a particular way the significance of the cognitive component in what is essentially a commonplace linguistic act - the telling of a personal experience to a sympathetic listener. One valid way of analyzing the tale is to suggest that the speaker works out his interpretation of the event with fair success: he is economical, clear, interesting. He operates well within the combination of gossip, narrative and drama and is at home, therefore, within the conventions of his chosen form. And he is linguistically fully competent for his purposes. But *if* one is keen to use the anecdote as an opportunity for moral education (and again, it does not have to be so used) it is the cognitive component that is central, and the development would lie in the refashioning of what the teller knows so well as to take for granted. It should be added that the tale was told as part of a session with a small group of poor readers in an English lesson. Using the methods of the 'Breakthrough to Literacy' project, the children were telling stories about themselves and dictating them to the teacher for the teacher to dictate back to the children.

The following can be offered as a contrast. It is a story written by a thirteen-year old for his English teacher.

> *Sundip was a quiet boy. He was 15 years old and lived with his parents and one younger brother called Nilesh.*
>
> *One Saturday morning he got up earlier than usual, went downstairs and made some breakfast. After breakfast he went up to call his mother, as Nilesh was crying. His mother told him, as he had woken up so early, he could knock for his friend, Raju, and then they could go to the morning show, as it was Saturday. So Sundip got ready and set off to his friend's house. When he got to Raju's gate, Raju was just coming out. 'I was just coming to knock for you, Sundip,' he said. 'So was I,' said Sundip. 'My mother said we could go to the morning show together,' said Raju.*
>
> *After a while, Raju came out and they both set off to the cinema. When they arrived there they saw a bunch of bullies standing outside and one of them was beating up a small Indian kid. They pretended*

they hadn't seen them and kept on looking straight ahead. Suddenly, one of the boys shouted, 'Look at them Pakis across the street!'
When Raju heard this he ran, and so Sundip was left alone. Sundip also ran but he was caught, and Raju managed to escape. Then a tall skinny boy, whose hair was half-dyed in yellow and half-dyed in green, said, 'You got any money on you, sonny?' Then another boy held his hair and pulled it so hard that it made Sundip's eyes water. 'He said have you got any money?'
Sundip put his hands in his pocket to reach out for 50p, which was the price of the ticket. 'N - n - no,' he said. And then he said, 'I forgot about that 50p.'
'I don't like you, and you wouldn't like what I do with the likes of you,' said the boy, who then leaned him up against a wall and punched him in the stomach. Sundip didn't like what they were doing one little bit. Then Sundip gave the boy a slight push but this meant trouble. The boy took off his leather jacket and pushed the other boys aside. Then he pulled Sundip towards him and slapped him across the face. 'If it's a fight you want, you get it,' said the boy. Sundip could hardly speak because he was hurt so bad. Then Sundip said in a soft voice, 'Please leave me alone, please!' He had never felt so hopeless in his whole life. At that time there were no adults, so the boy was really beating Sundip up. There were all large bruises and bumps and Sundip was bleeding all over. Then suddenly the boys heard the sound of a police car siren, so they ran, and the boy with the dyed hair got his jacket and he ran too. There were two police cars, one of them saw the boys running and chased them. The other car had Raju inside, and as soon as the police car stopped, Raju ran out to see his friend. As soon as he saw him, tears ran down his cheeks. It was the first time he'd ever cried in public. He couldn't believe it. His own friend was lying half dead on the road. Then the siren of an ambulance was heard, and soon Sundip laid on a stretcher and was taken to hospital.
When Sundip's mother heard this, she screamed. She couldn't understand why they had beaten up a boy who didn't mean any harm. After a few days, the doctor told Mrs Patel, Sundip's mother that he was going to be all right. He had just broken an arm and a leg, but he needed a lot of rest. And the police said that the boys were all caught and taken to jail for 18 months.

This writer, unlike the previous story-teller, sees justice residing in the forces of law and order. The police arrive in the nick of time, and justice prevails. Likewise, the adult society in general is seen as protective. It is because there are no adults around that the thugs take action. The writer also assumes that he or his protagonist is vulnerable to the point of offering no resistance to the enemy; his modest steps at resisting or hitting back are half-hearted and soon abandoned. Compare, too, the role of the mother in the two stories. Here the mother screams and then puzzles over the perversity of the enemy. The mother from the previous story would have jumped into her car and pursued the foe in person.

In effect, the underlying values of the two boys are different in certain vital respects, and are contained within those things which they know so well that they do not need saying, and which they also assume the reader or listener does not need telling. And the person who seeks to change these values in any way is initiating a complex task. (A good place to begin would be to set up opportunities for the two boys to exchange stories and talk about them!) The problem is intrinsic to learning (and teaching) of all kinds, but most vividly so in those areas where human affairs are the direct focus of attention.

The Problem of Evidence

There is a third kind of assumption which plays a similarly major role in learning, and this is concerned not with what is good or worthwhile (values) but with *what needs to be proved.* Thus the historian does not generally demand verification of William I's activities in 1066; nor does the sociologist of Marx's authorship of *'Capital'*; nor does the scientist of the law of gravity. At some stage or other such matters are established as beyond dispute by the adherents of the subject and are then made the basis for further additions to the territory of the indisputable.

A student coming new to any topic or subject does not know what the appropriate assumptions are. The student's teacher, however, is deeply imbued with these assumptions, and has to make a major intellectual act of going back to the beginning and helping the learner to come to terms with them. But in doing so, the teacher can never quite shake off what is so fundamentally taken for granted by those 'in the know'. More important, the student is well aware that the teacher is pretending to be ignorant, and that the teacher generally knows the answers to the questions that are asked (by the teacher or by the student). One consequence of this is that the student is eager to start joining in the game and to make assumptions too.

Consider, for example, this piece of work by a 12-year-old in his first year at secondary school, writing an account in *science* of practical work carried out in the laboratory:

THE DISTILLATION OF IMPURE WATER

We lit our bunsen burner under a flask which had dirty water in, gradually the dirty water boiled and it obviously produced steam. The steam had to expand but the top of the flask was blocked by a cork but in the side of the flask was a tube so the steam escaped through the tube and travelled down into a beaker which turned the dirty water in-

to clean water. Our water from which we started off was dirty and the object of our experiment was to turn the impure water into pure water. As you maybe know steam is really water and is also pure so that is how we got our pure water from the impure water. The steam which went through the tube was very hot and because of this we were getting less water in the beaker and more steam, so we connected two rubber tubes one tube was taking the water from a tap (oh yes around the tube was a water jacket I will explain about this more) into the water jacket. Which on the other side of the water jacket was another rubber tube which was collecting the water from the water jacket. So the water cooled the steam down and this helped to produce more water and much less steam. On our bunsen burner should be a blue flame under the flask but it is no longer needed so we can turn it down a bit because we might get too much steam and this will produce more water than we are in need of. From this experiment we can conclude that we can extract pure H_2O from impure H_2O also on cooling steam (gas) water (liquid) is obtained. The water jacket is used to cool the steam down and it helps to produce more water and less steam.

The writer handles a wide range of ideas; he uses some very complex structures within certain sentences (including a bracketed aside inserted into the middle of a clause); and he achieves considerable precision at certain points in his thinking, as with - 'as you may know steam is really water and is also pure so that is how we get our pure water from the impure water.' But one valid follow-up for this particular pupil might well be to invite him to talk about other kinds of possible evidence. For example, what other ways are there to demonstrate the same idea? What is the evidence that the idea is itself of any importance? What is the evidence for the proposition that dirty and clean water are two different things? And could we restage the evidence he uses here to spell out each stage in simple detail? Could he explain the evidence to somebody who is *not* in any sense a scientist?

In effect, the work as written assumes that the evidence is conclusive and that the need for the experiment is itself self-evident. This by no means invalidates the work, but simply points the way for a possible next step.

Without such assumptions neither the general nor the specialized use of knowledge would be possible. Not even the most popular cf newspapers could function without them. But these assumptions constitute the most formidable barrier for the learner, and attempts to 'begin at the beginning', to go 'back to basics', to make everything very simple indeed, do not necessarily do anything of the kind. For they may do nothing to unravel or clarify those assumptions which the learner is not able to make. This is one of the major reasons for encouraging learners to work together and talk together and ask their own questions.

The Ways We Think

A second group of problems pertain to the ways in which we think. Whenever we think anything out, no matter how briskly or ordinarily, we engage in a creative act: we fashion something new. In doing so, we work our ways through a number of conflicts, each generating its own tension.

1. We seek to be economical, while also to be precise.
2. We seek to express ourselves, to be creative, while also being correct enough to make sense to others.
3. We seek to attend to the whole of the task without losing sight of it in its component parts and to attend to each part without losing sight of it in the whole.

These different tensions are present in some measure throughout our thinking and create distinct problems of their own.

The Problem of Economy Versus Precision

To create something that is meaningful is partly a matter of the elimination of uncertainties and ambiguities. Simultaneously, time is a factor also, even in the most liberal of circumstances. We are always looking forward to the end - whether we are reading a book or writing one, or listening to a lecture or giving one, or wrestling with a problem in mathematics. Hence, we are constantly aiming not to repeat ourselves, not to beat about the bush, not to charge around the houses. And the two activities - getting it clear and precise, and getting it over and done with - always, to some extent, conflict with each. Precision leads us into qualification and elaboration. Economy urges us to conclude. In the classroom this tension cannot be abolished, but the teacher can at least be aware of the problem, and, at least some of the time, place the emphasis on one side of the process rather than the other.

What follows is an example of children seeking to achieve very considerable economy *and* precision in a single activity. They are 15-year-olds and have been working with their English teacher on the art and the craft of writing for newspapers. They have looked, among other things, at the ways in which journalists organize their information and the ways in which they move from one 'fact' to the next. One of their assignments has been to interview, as a class, a visiting American educationist, and then to write up their reports as if for a newspaper. Here are three short extracts from three different pieces, in each case taken from the opening of the finished reports.

1. Mrs Marion Cardwell, reading specialist and adviser to the schools of New Jersey, U.S.A. yesterday visited a London comprehensive school and spoke to a group of 15-year-olds about teaching methods in America.
   She began by pointing out that teachers in America are much more

well educated than those in England, because they spend more time training (4 to 5 years) and must obtain more qualifications. . . .

2. British schools are 15 years behind American schools! This claim was made by Mrs Marion Cardwell, a reading specialist from New Jersey, while visiting Murrays Comprehensive School on Wednesday. Mrs Cardwell has been touring Great Britain to see the way reading is taught here compared to New Jersey. . . .

3. Mrs Marion Cardwell, a reading specialist and an adviser to the schools of New Jersey, was interviewed by Tony Marks, a reporter for this paper yesterday. Mrs Cardwell has been touring this country looking at British schools. She was not impressed. . . .

All three reports are remarkably economical, able to capture a number of basic points in a very limited space: Cardwell is a reading specialist from New Jersey; has told a London comprehensive school about her impressions of teaching methods in Britain; and is very critical of what she has seen. All three have made an excellent job of finding a precise and unambiguous way of reporting all this in very few words. Possibly, the second is the most precise of all, in that it directs us from the very start to the key point with which the other two also are concerned, but which they need to introduce more fully. In this way too, the second is closer to the conventions of the newspaper report. It is also the second writer who makes clear that Cardwell is looking at reading methods rather than teaching methods in general. By contrast, the writer of the following excerpt is to a fair extent overwhelmed in her attempt to be precise. She is 16 years of age, and has written for her English teacher about whether it is better to leave school at 15 or 16.

I think that 16 is the right age to leave because then you are treated as an adult and you could get a job. But if you left school when you were 16 or 15 you still have to have exams. I think you should have exams but only English and Maths, because I think they are more important than the other subjects because for example, take shop work. You need maths and English to know what to do, and in metalwork or woodwork you still need Maths. Now Mrs Thatcher is Prime Minister she said that children who is 15 could leave school only if they have a job but the people who leave school when they're 16 won't be able to get a job because 15 year olds have already got them. I think that 15 is a right age to leave because then you can get a job but when they left in the old days they were 15 and 14 only to get a job to help to feed your families because your parents would be at work to get money to feed the family. Nowadays its only the Dads go to work. Sometimes both parents go to work. This is why the children are leaving at 16. I think the good advantages is that when you are 16 you have exams then leaving school finding a job. . . .

Whereas the writers of the news reports have been able to achieve considerable economy and precision within the form they are working in, this piece of discursive writing would probably be helped by the chance to chat and discuss and to break out of the written discursive form altogether. She makes some excellent points, not least in showing the paradox of a decision to release some children at age 15, thereby reducing the jobs market for those who leave at 16. And she begins to explore some useful contrasts with earlier times, but she desperately needs the second or third voices of friends, asking, 'What do you mean by . . .? Do you think . . . But you said just now. . . .' She might then also be less economical, and take her time to work out what she means.

The Problem of Creativity Versus Correctness

Whenever we use language we to some degree commit ourselves, engage in a creative improvisation. We are not necessarily, therefore, by any objective standpoint original, though we may sometimes be very original indeed by our own standards, but we are nevertheless *creative*. There is something about the particular way we have worked out our task that is specifically our own. The three children writing up their news report on the lady from New Jersey are all creative, all different from one another. The divergent thinkers among us are in one sense more creative, or highly creative, but even the convergers are moving at some point in the same direction: finding their own meaning, creating their own language.

Our creativity always operates within certain constraints, imposed by our sense of what others will understand or accept as appropriate to the form in which we are working. There is a sense in which work which we do not in any way intend others to see is freed from such constraints, but even here we may well have in mind some kind of internalized audience, no matter how friendly, and edit our work accordingly.

Of course many teachers engage their children in highly creative endeavour, and they do this at least in part by creating the kind of warm and appreciative audience for the children's work in which the learner can feel both secure and adventurous. Even then, for the learner, there is still a certain tension between the two needs, and hence a certain contradiction: the need to be 'correct' and the need to be 'creative'.

One consequence of this is the neat, tidy, 'correct' and yet very unimaginative work which scores acceptable, and sometimes high, marks in examinations. All the candidates are doing is working out what is required of them and delivering the goods down to the final word. Yet, ironically enough, examination boards endlessly complain that they are presented with candidates' work in which originality and commitment are conspicuous for their absence. Moreover, even when we actually ask someone to be creative, to 'write what you like' or 'just have fun with paint', we really mean something far more specific and restrictive than we claim, and are interpreted accordingly by the other person.

The Problem of The Whole Versus the Parts

Meaning is made as we move forwards and then backwards from the whole to the part to the whole again, and yet back again, repeating the process many times. Finding a place on the map means much more than simply finding *that* place. It means locating the place in relation to many others and in many different kinds of relationship. The same applies to reading a word, or a sentence or a book. It applies also to talking, where we constantly focus on 'parts' and then seek to bring them together into 'wholes'. It applies also to writing. In the case of writing, we are perhaps most especially surrounded by 'parts' - having to contend not only with the meaning of what we are writing but also with the various devices that enable others to share our meaning, such as punctuation, spelling and legible handwriting.

Life, or at least learning, is rendered more difficult by the fact that we do not at first know the difference between the part and the whole; part of the process of learning is one of finding links, turning 'many' into 'one', and likewise of breaking one down into many and then joining them together again with something else.

Part of the complexity of teaching is in knowing *when* to ask people to make such links and of knowing what the particular links are. J. S. Bruner's famous theory of the 'spiral curriculum' is related to this problem, and in part asserts that in learning we are able to make more links as we go along, and thus that there is an important place in a curriculum for preliminary encounters, return visits, and so on. In other words, it is important for children to meet different concepts repeatedly, penetrating their complexity a little at a time, working on them at a variety of different levels.

One important corollary to Bruner's idea of the 'spiral curriculum' is that return visits, to roughly familiar material, need to be built into the curriculum rather than be left to arise unscheduled. At the moment, for instance, secondary schools are largely unaware of the particular work pursued in their feeder primary schools, and where the secondary curriculum picks up topics already explored in the primary there is very little real connection established. In a sense, neither school is using the work of the other, and the child's education is itself the poorer for this.

We give some particular examples of children wrestling with this problem of making links, of joining parts together, and breaking things down into their component parts, in the context of children reading - in Chapters 5 and 6.

The Ways We Work

An exploration of the problems attaching to the specific ways in which pupils work, and are asked to work, is outlined in the later chapters devoted to the teaching of talking, reading and writing. In particular our attempts to spell out the roles of the teacher in each of these activities are also attempts to isolate the kinds of problems which children face in the actual *ways in which they work,* and which are to a large degree independent of what they know, or of their capacity to think, or of the language they use. These problems seem essentially to be of three kinds.

A Lack of Models

Very often children cannot work in a particular way, because they have not had the chance to internalize models of that particular way of working. Perhaps they have never seen group discussions of problems, for example, or taken part in them. Perhaps they have little, if any, experience of tracking down information in a reference library and of then using the information for some other purpose. Perhaps they have no experience of working out ideas by way of a series of preliminary ventures, rough drafts and so on. Or they may have no awareness, again due to lack of experience, of referring back to work that has been done previously in order to build upon it now.

In lacking models to internalize, they also lack in many cases any advice as to the component features from which to construct their own models. Thus the teacher needs to be willing to spell out to children the various techniques that they are to use - whether it be in the running of a discussion, the planning of an essay, or the use of various sources of evidence in the writing of a speech for a debate.

Preliminary Work

Difficulties can also arise because children are not clearly and explicitly encouraged to make notes, prepare rough drafts, revise what they do, and use what they have done already as a basis for further work. This is not to say that final drafts have no place, for they obviously have.

Lack of Variety

A further source of problems is the repetition of the same kind of work over a long period, or in other words, a lack of variety in the work. Endless reading and writing; endless listening; endless talking - all lack of variety is conducive to poor work, for it weakens stamina and interest and motivation. Numerous official reports have drawn attention to the problem of school curricula which fail to observe this common sense principle. Secondary schools in particular are likely to deceive themselves that by changing *subjects* at regular intervals in the course of a school day so they also change the *activity* in which the child is expected to engage. In fact, though, the child may be asked to do the same kind of activity from one subject to the next.

The Language We Use
Finally, a number of problems relate to the use of the language itself.

The Problem of Correctness
Teachers have traditionally devoted a lot of their time and energy to correcting children's language. Such corrections can themselves be confusing, for they can cover quite different kinds of mistake. There is first, the *mistake of fact,* as when a date is wrongly reported, or a character is allocated to the wrong novel. There is secondly, a mistake in the way in which any problem or task is *thought out.* For example, a statement may be so imprecise as to be ambiguous, or it may be concerned with only a part of a problem, or it may be very brief, when a detailed piece of work was asked for. In the case of the written language such mistakes may consist entirely of poor punctuation which in turn may render what is written virtually incomprehensible or at the very least, ambiguous. Thirdly, there is the mistake that comes from a *misuse of a register,* as when a formal letter of application for employment is couched in the terms of a friendly letter home. Into this category come many of the common errors in writing, where the writer employs the language of everyday speech inappropriately in a formal literary register. An example would be the use of a double negative in a discursive essay, or the use of colloquialisms such as 'ain't', or the mixing of singular and plural forms, as when Mark says in the discussion on Castro's Cuba (quoted in the previous chapter at line 73) - 'They was all captured. . . .'

Most people, and not only teachers, tend to think of many of the conventions of written registers as absolute rules, but they seldom are. Spelling for instance, tends to vary between England and the U.S.A. Even punctuation varies in certain registers, and, for example, some novelists appear to rewrite the rules for using full-stops. And for certain kinds of documents drawn up by lawyers, the convention is to use no punctuation whatsoever.

Fourthly, there is the mistake that is essentially a *misuse of the language itself,* which in effect means that the user invents his or her own language, however briefly. The child who writes 'prettiful' instead of 'pretty', or who say 'brunged' instead of 'brought', is making such a mistake, though it is perfectly possible that the mistake could be one of register, rather than of language itself, for such words might well come from an accurate copying of words used in stories or entertainments. Invented spellings, whether imaginative or otherwise, fall in the same category. It is worth adding, however, that many mistakes in all four categories are not fatal to the meaning of what is said or written.

The kind of mistake that is made then can be of any of these four kinds, and it is important for the teacher to know what kind of mistake he or she is looking at or hearing. Then the child can be helped to see the nature of the mistake also. Obviously there will be many times when any particular mistake is not high on the list of priorities for present action, but when it is, it can be dangerous to misrepresent what the child has done. As a popular example, it is highly misleading to correct the child who writes, 'We was . . .' with the advice that this is not English, or even that it is not good English, whatever that may mean. It is more simply a use of language that is not used in certain situations, but is used in others.

The Problem of Written Language

We have already stressed, in our analysis of the group discussion in the first chapter, that the written and the spoken language are not identical. The language of everyday conversation is elliptical, full·of omissions, deeply connected to bodily movement and gesture, and often different on a basic grammatical level from written language. Much of the time, for instance, we do not speak in sentences, and even less do we speak in sentences that explicitly relate to each other. Children have to master this confusing difference and all that it entails, and there is always a danger that in doing so they will be expected to operate entirely in the written language and to leave their spoken language outside the classroom. Similarly, they may be expected to make a simple transition from speech to writing and quite often somebody else's speech into their own writing.

The Problem of Linguistic Complexity

The idea of linguistic complexity has recently become a popular topic in educational circles - and rightly so. Generally it is equated with the idea of length: language becomes more complex (and hence more daunting to the learner) as passages become longer, as sentences become longer, and as words become longer. Reading ages, reading-difficulty scores, and all kinds of reading tests to some degree employ the notion of length of the unit of utterance as an indicator of its complexity. We accept this idea in a broad or general sense, while adding that the complexity of any piece of language for any reader or listener, is also related to a number of other factors, including acquaintance with the subject-matter and the particular ways in which the user of language thinks about his or her task. In short, the complexity of the language unto itself is only one aspect of its overall complexity. In our later chapters on Reading we give specific illustrations of this.

The Problem of Register

Good teachers provide varied opportunities to children to internalize different registers even within one subject. This itself makes demands on the child's ability to get the register 'right'. This means not only knowing the conventions, or getting to know the conventions, but also extending your command of the subject-matter to encompass a new register. For, in effect, even within a single topic, change of register involves change of knowledge. What you need to know in order to write a discursive essay about Cleopatra is not at all the same as you need to know in order to write a short story about her.

Registers in Writing History

Consider for example the difficulties encountered by the boy who has written the following for his history teacher. The work was set after a lesson discussing Hadrian's Wall and was in the context of a series of lessons concerned with the Roman occupation of Britain. As part of the work the class read W. H. Auden's *Roman Wall Blues.* They were then asked, among other tasks, to write a letter from a Roman soldier posted on the Wall. This is the letter written by one of the boys; he is 11 years old.

January IX, CXXXV A.D.
Housestead's Fort,
Hadrian's Wall,
Britain.

Dear Mum and Dad,

How are you. I aint feeling very well myself. I have been walking around all day to report what happened in the battle, and how much damage as been caused. I really do wish I was back at home enjoying myself like you are doing. This draughty mile block that I am in every day for at least 15 hours gives me all my colds I get. Last week we spent a whole day trying to drive away mad Scotchmen and Picts. We finally succeeded but I was not at all pleased, since I see the army coming and was not hurt I had to report all damage and how many people had been killed. I finally got to put my feet up and was awarded extra wages for the marvellous job I had done sending signal all day and night. In about 12 weeks we shall be celebrating my birthday. You may come if you wish but you must wear a green top and the rest must be red, and if you wear a hat it must have a white band on it with a red feather sticking out. If you come and are not in these special colours the lookout men will mistake you for intruders and proberly kill you. Still my birthday is still a good three months away so you need not worry about it yet.

We get good food and exelent wine we are treated fair anoth. But accasionaly we are treated very badly. There is not anoth go round and sometimes people fight over the grub. But being of such a high quallity the food servers always make sure I get a good share of wine and food. Soldiers are forever gambling and losing valuable rings and necklesses. Some soldiers even bet their lives if they are certain they will win. But unfortunately some come unstuck and loose their lives. Still I must go now, bye bye

Love
Julius Pontius

P.S. I'll write next month.

One of the interests of the piece is the way in which the boy's imaginative (and wholly commendable) attempt to get inside the character of an historical figure leads him outside and beyond the knowledge he has acquired so far in the history lessons. At points he seems to be replacing what he has already learned with knowledge that is more personal and familiar to him. Thus he writes of the draughty mile 'block' and not of the 'castle'. Presumably he is thinking of the blocks of classrooms in the school he goes to, or perhaps he is thinking of prison blocks that he has seen in films or on television. Later he suggests the strange device of wearing a silly hat in order to avoid being mistaken for the enemy, though the history teacher on this occasion can recall no discussion of any such phenomenon in this context. Likewise, the intrusion of the birthday suggests the force of a very personal consideration that very much preoccupies the writer. It leads him into a certain lack of perspective both historically and geographically. The family are unlikely to make the trek across Europe for a birthday celebration at that particular time in history, and, if they do, they are unlikely to be mistaken for Picts, as they will presumably approach from the south. Later, there is the intriguing (and probably incorrect) assumption that Roman soldiers would wear necklaces.

There are opportunities too, to utilize knowledge that has been acquired during previous lessons, and which the writer ignores. He refers to signalling between the mile castles but makes no reference to the methods employed, which were discussed previously in class. He does not describe the Picts, and he does not give any details of the maltreatment of the soldiers, though he touches on this in a general way. Both topics had been explored with all the pupils.

Hence, as part of a sequence of activities, such a task performs a valuable exercise: it helps the child to explore something of the subjective reality of history, and it helps the teacher to see some of the gaps in the child's knowledge that are relevant to understanding the subject in question. This gives both teacher and taught an important point of departure for further work, whereas a short, sharp test of a factual nature might be not only less creative for the child but also less useful to the teacher.

Summary

We have suggested that a number of problems arise in learning, and that the teacher can help the learner to 'get it right' by distinguishing these problems from each other:

The Problem of the Knowledge on Which the Learner Draws

1. In determining what is *relevant* and irrelevant to a given task, there is the danger that the learner will rule out of consideration a great deal of prior experience, such that he or she is left with nothing on which to build.
2. The learner's values may be so invisible to the learner, that there is no chance of a rethinking or reconsideration of those values.
3. The learner may absorb new knowledge without examining the evidence for it, rapidly accepting the assumptions on which *teaching* is based without in any sense understanding them.

Problems Arising from The Ways in Which the Learner Thinks

4. The urge to be reasonably precise while also being fairly economical.
5. The need to be expressive or creative, while also being correct.
6. The difficulty of relating the parts of a problem to the whole, and the whole to the parts.

Problems Arising from The Ways in Which The Learner Sets to Work

7. A lack of clear models on how to work in any given way.
8. A lack of opportunities to make notes, and in various ways, to engage in preliminary work.
9. A lack of variety in the activities themselves.

Problems Arising from The Learner's Use of Language

10. Identifying the different kinds of mistakes that are made.
11. Moving too rapidly from spoken to written language, or indeed neglecting discursive talk in the classroom. This is an aspect of the problem of registers, and of children having opportunities to internalize models of all the registers in which they are asked to work.

12. The complexity of the language itself.

We now have a broad framework with which to explore the learner's problems and the teacher's role right across the central activities of language and learning in the classroom: talking, reading and writing.

In the next chapter, we look at the teacher's role in group discussions.

3
Group Discussion: The Teacher's Role

Introduction

In the first chapter we gave a transcript and evaluation of the group discussion on Castro's Cuba. We will refer back to that discussion in outlining different aspects of the teacher's role. What does the teacher do? What is the teacher's responsibility?

Perhaps the question that precedes either of these is the more basic: *how does the teacher know what has been happening?* Unlike a piece of written work it is not 'there', waiting to be marked. To the contrary, a group discussion evaporates even as it is happening. Occasionally, of course, the teacher will do what we have done here and ask the students to tape their discussions. Perhaps the tape will be played back to the class. Perhaps the teacher will make a transcript of it and read this with the class and discuss it. (Obviously there will be times when the teacher will judge this to be inappropriate.) Alternatively, the teacher may ask the group to make notes while they are talking and to report back, using their notes, to the whole class. Or they may be asked to produce some sustained piece of writing. In one or other of these ways, the teacher learns something of what has happened and seeks to build upon it.

Ways of Working

In effect, there are two sides to the teacher's role as an organizer of the children's work: first initiating group activity, and then helping the children to become more sophisticated and confident members of the groups.

Setting up Groups

How do teachers set up groups? And how do they change a group's dynamics to give everyone a chance to contribute? And how do they handle the situation where someone does not want to work with any group (the isolate) or alternatively is not wanted by any group (the reject)?

The temptation is for the teacher to decide who works with whom, and to spend a lot of time and energy on allocating everyone to their proper place. This is generally a mistake. The best groups are self-chosen: the teacher specifies the task, and the groups choose themselves. In the early stages of such work, it can be useful even to decree that the groups should choose themselves more or less from where they are sitting in the classroom.

The groups' task needs to be clearly defined beforehand, not least because the composition of the groups will itself depend upon the nature of the assignment. One technique available to the teacher who finds that certain students get left out of all the groups, is to introduce a quite different type of assignment next time round - for instance one involving detailed use of the library, or the employment of a secretary who takes minutes, and so on. As the assignments change, so, in time, will the composition of the groups.

If this does not help to resolve the dilemma of the excluded individuals, there is also the device of asking group X to assimilate somebody else, or even of rearranging a number of other groups in order to effect the same purpose. In effect the mature members of the class will be able to assimilate newcomers without great effort, but in this, as in all things, practice makes us better (if not perfect). If someone really prefers to work alone, then, at least, for some occasions this may well be the right thing to do. Again, everything will depend on the sequencing of the activities, of new assignments, of new chances to work together. Indeed once group work appears to be going well, there is a lot to be said for deliberately encouraging a greater social mix in the classroom, as when the teacher asks a pair from one group to report their findings to a pair from another group. And the teacher can help to set the right example by himself or herself spending time with a different group at different occasions.

Learning the Conventions

Learning to discuss problems together is partly a matter of learning the various rules of the game and the possible variations of the game. Hence, one of the teacher's aims is to encourage the children's own interest in the whole *idea of talk and discussion*. One way of doing this is by talking about the ways in which a discussion has progressed and about the problems encountered, and perhaps even the techniques that are useful in encouraging good contributions from one another. A further technique is for the teacher literally to *change the conventions* by which the groups work on the next occasion. We have already mentioned the idea of asking the students to keep brief notes of main points raised. At some times it may be helpful for one student to keep very detailed notes which the whole group later adapt into complete minutes of the discussion for presentation to the whole class. It would be helpful for Harry's group, for example, to work without any kind of text-book and then compare results - Is the text-book useful? How could it be used more effectively?

Harry's group shows enough cohesiveness to be able to adapt to change in the membership of the group. They could, for instance, be asked to divide into two groups to work on some follow-up project with other groups in the class, similarly divided and regrouped. In this way, it is possible that someone like Philip will come to play a more positive role. Indeed, the social psychologists argue that is is only by creating new opportunities to work with people that such qualities can be developed. It could well be, for example, that Philip is over-awed by the prowess of Harry, and that he will only become more of a leader in a group where Harry is not a member.

The Problem of Noise

Teachers have a high regard for silence, and so do school principals. Talking is a form of noise, and it can, especially in small groups, generate a great deal of noise. Sometimes the noise becomes so great that nobody can hear anybody else.

There can be no simple answer. Most classrooms are poorly designed acoustically, and indeed in most schools the noise made by teachers is distracting to other teachers, let alone the noise made by students. All we can do is seek to be tolerant of each other; encourage students to talk as quietly as possible; perhaps encourage short bursts of group talk and extend the time as the aptitude increases; and generally encourage the convention that we can talk about something together without raising the roof. But roofs do need to be raised from time to time. That, too, is a part of the basic structure of discussion.

Ways of Thinking

One of the teacher's contributions may be to suggest to the children some of the *different strategies* they can adopt. For example, Harry's group could be asked to explore a 'factor' approach to the Cuban problem, examining the political, geographical, economic and military factors that affect the relationship between the two countries. Or they might be asked to note especially the points on which they *cannot agree* or to which they think there is no real answer. Or they might be asked to consider some totally new aspect of the problem, and to examine its relevance, if any. They might be given, say, a set of trade figures showing the commercial inter-dependence of Cuba and the U.S.A. in the 5 years before Castro's revolution, and asked to discuss their significance.

Perhaps too the teacher will spend time with each group, and on occasions will contribute the kinds of questions which may help to move their thinking towards greater precision, or greater divergence, or towards some new aspect of the problem - whatever the teacher thinks appropriate.

The Knowledge Used

Discussion is the ideal context for bringing together a range of knowledge in the study of some kind of problem. Perhaps the teacher will specifically introduce some new kind of information specifically for group discussion, in the way we have just indicated above. Or he may precede the discussion with a revision of all the various points that are related to the problem. Or there may well be a value in using the group discussion as a means of first engaging in such revision, with the group preparing a short factual test to be given to other groups. It may also be useful on occasions to have group discussion of ways in which knowledge drawn from outside a specific subject may be incorporated into the study of a particular problem.

The Language Used

What is the teacher's role in helping the children to extend and develop their language within the context of a group discussion? Obviously, working together, thinking things out, extending the fields of knowledge with which they are familiar - all these become part of their language development. But to what extent can we talk of group discussion as aiding language development specifically? We can highlight four ways in which the teacher can play a useful role.

First, as people talk together, they in various ways *internalize the language of the group.* Hence, there is an important place for varied opportunities not only to work in groups, but also to work in different groups. Again, the best way to do this is to set up groups to do different kinds of things, to vary the nature of the task. The more we work with different people, the more widely can language develop. Hence, too, there is an important place for opportunities not only to change groups but also to change class - to work with quite different people at different times.

It is not only the membership of the group that affects the language used, -there is also the *material on which the group work.* For example, a group who read a passage together and talk about it, are often able to do useful work with material that is too complex for some, or even all, of the group. Hence, the various members of the group are able to internalize literature that might otherwise be inaccessible to them. This is a point to which we turn later in the chapters on Reading. Also relevant is the *type of project* itself. For example, using a group discussion to help prepare speeches for debate, and on another occasion to help prepare a discursive essay, and on another occasion to help prepare a newspaper report - variations of these kinds in the project itself will all help the children to internalize different kinds of language, different registers and hence promote their language development. Finally, the *involvement of teachers* themselves, as sympathetic listeners and occasional contributors, can also provide new models for the children's language.

Development in Group Discussion

Children learn to discuss together by discussing together. Discussion is a fundamental use of language, just as listening to a story is, or telling one. At all stages in their development, children can and do discuss together.

How, then, does discussion develop? It does so in a number of ways all of which have their equivalent place in the development of children's reading and writing. As children advance through the school, so they extend the *range of knowledge* on which they can draw in their discussions. They literally know more. Hence they are able to widen their sense of what is and what is not relevant. At the same time, their sense of what is irrelevant inevitably deepens at the same pace, and so they become increasingly knowledgeable while also increasingly editorial in their thinking. In other words, their *thinking* changes also. They are capable of greater economy and greater precision because they have more experience on which to base their thinking. They can thus relate more 'parts' to one another to create new 'wholes', finding links they could not have found before. But again, this is not purely a liberating process, for they are increasingly caught in the tension between economy and precision, and between creativity and correctness; learning is in some measure an inhibiting experience, bringing with it a discipline and organization of thinking.

As they discuss, so they also extend their *language,* mastering more complex grammatical forms and being able to hold forth at greater length, to listen for longer periods of time, and participate in more extended conversations. They are also able to *work* successfully in different groups, increasingly able to join new groups and to absorb newcomers into their own groups.

All children are developing at some point or other of this rough sequence we have just outlined. But their development is not a simple, linear progress. In other words, their skill in working as a group is not independent of the task at hand, or of the subject-matter, or of the ways in which they are asked to work out a given problem. At its simplest, we are not able to discuss something about which we know nothing. Any one of the four dimensions - knowledge, thinking, working, language - may be out of step with the others at any particular time or in any particular task.

The teacher's use of group discussion is of course intrinsically related to the teacher's use of class discussion, and it is to this which we must now turn. We will then seek to compare the teacher's role in both activities.

4

Class Discussion:
The Teacher's Role

Introduction

How far do different considerations apply to discussion in the class as a single unit?

As a way of providing a starting-point and a contrast, we give here an extract from a class discussion, where a science teacher is working with a class of 11-year-olds. The teacher is planning to give a series of lessons on evolution. Here the teacher introduces the topic by asking the children to talk about what they already know. His aim is to involve the children in asking questions together, to help him, as the teacher, see where he goes from here, and in general to lay the foundation for the next few lessons.

As before, we are not in any way claiming that this is a typically good or typically bad example of a class discussion. All it does is offer some evidence of what goes on when teacher and class come together to discuss.

Class Discussion

Teacher:	*. . . So we're just chatting about what we know already. Who'd like to start us off? Rajinder?*
Rajinder:	*Sir, the first animals were amphibians.*
Teacher:	*Mm. Meaning what, Rajinder?*
Rajinder:	*Sir, they live on land or in the sea.* (5)
Teacher:	*Mm. Good.*
Parvin:	*And the dinosaurs.*
Teacher:	*Yes. What about the dinosaurs, Parvin?*
Parvin:	*Sir, they were big creatures that . . . (inaudible)*
Bill:	*Sir, scientists think that the earth started to evolve in the* (10) *sea, by tiny creatures who developed lungs and came up to the earth. Came to the ground and started to grow bigger. And started to live on land.*
Teacher:	*Good . . . Colin?*
Colin:	*The first things who lived on land were trees and plants.* (15)

Teacher:	*The first living things?*
Colin:	*Trees and plants, all over the world. And the sea evolved.*
Teacher:	*Very interesting. Any other suggestions?*
George:	*Scientists discovered that the dinosaurs disappeared.*
Teacher:	*Just out of interest, any ideas about how we know that* (20) *there were dinosaurs? After all, we weren't around to take photographs of them.*
George:	*Archaeologists digging up, they found bones and all that, fossils.*
Teacher:	*Good.* (25)
George:	*And stones. And they put them in museums so people could see what happened before them.*
Teacher:	*Like to explain, George, what a fossil is?*
George:	*It's a stone, Sir, It's small and goes round and round.*
Teacher:	*Good. And how do scientists know, or reckon they know,* (30) *that fossils are so old?*
Dean:	*Sir, they're given chemical tests.*
Teacher:	*Good. Would anybody like to add to that?*
Henry:	*They found the shapes in rocks, and the only way the rocks could have formed over them was over a lot of years.* (35)
Teacher:	*Very good. Excellent.*
Colin:	*From the depth they are under the ground.*
Teacher:	*Very good.*
Bill:	*Say you've got something in the water, like a dolphin. If it died it would land in water so nobody else - the water would* (40) *disappear and all the earth would grow above it. And they can tell how old it is by how much the earth covers it.*
Teacher:	*I see. Very interesting. Any other comments on it?*
Bill:	*Sir, another thing that explains how fossils came about is the mystery of the Tollund Man.* (45)
Teacher:	*Mm?*
Bill:	*This man, Sir, he done something wrong, and he was left on the ground and put in a pit. And they put earth over him. And his body was preserved. And his fossil is his actual shape.* (50)
Teacher:	*Can you explain that again?*
Colin:	*They think he died from hanging. There was a rope round his neck.*
Teacher:	*And how old do they think this is?*
Colin:	*2000 years.* (55)
Bill:	*They think the man was in his early 20s.*
George:	*Sir, scientists even know what his last meal was.*
Teacher:	*Really?*

Arnold:	*Maybe the food was preserved in the stomach and they took some samples.* (60)
Teacher:	*And the stomach was well enough preserved?*
Steve:	*It was preserved in peat.*
Teacher:	*We've said something about dinosaurs and them disappearing. Anyone, any ideas about how this happened?*
Henry:	*Sir, did dinosaurs disappear because of the ice-age?* (65)
Teacher:	*Why? What happened then?*
Henry:	*It went from warm to cold and the dinosaurs couldn't stand it.*
Teacher:	*And what happened to other things in the ice-age?*
Henry:	*There weren't any men around.* (70)
Bill:	*There wasn't in the first ice-age. There was in the second ice-age.*
Teacher:	*Why do you reckon dinosaurs disappeared and men didn't, then?*
Niresh:	*Starvation.* (75)
Carl:	*They were warm-blooded, and so they died.*
Winston:	*Some of the animals . . .*
Vince:	*One reason is that the herbivores depended on the plants for their food, and the plants died out that they usually eat. And then they started to starve and died out. And then* (80) *the carnivores eat all the herbivores. So the meat-eaters had no more to rely on so they died out as well. So they killed each other.*
Teacher:	*That's a marvellous point to make. Can you just take us through it again?* (85)
Vince:	*Sir, the plants died out, so the herbivores starved and they died. And the carnivores depended on the herbivores for their food but they died out - so they died out as well.*
Arnold:	*Most of the animals were killed off by the humans.*
Bill:	*Sir, when the ice-age came all the plants died, so the herb-* (90) *ivores didn't have anything to eat, and they wouldn't eat each other so they died out.*
Teacher:	*There was a lot of very interesting ideas there. And we'll come back later to them. In the meantime, are there any questions you think you would like to ask? Questions that* (95) *you think we ought to try to answer while we are studying life on earth and how it all began?*
Vince:	*I don't understand scientists when they talk about the molecules growing larger.*
George:	*I don't understand what the Tollund Man did. What really* (100) *happened?*

Bill: *Sir, why did life start in the first place?*
Niresh: *If man could live, why couldn't dinosaurs live?*
Winston: *I don't understand - Why didn't one of the dinosaurs live*
           longer than the rest? Why didn't he live on the rest? (105)
Vince: *Why have all the early men got different names?*

Ways of Working

A number of features characterize the ways in which the class set to work on this activity.

A Dominating Member, Supported by the Class

All groups, large or small, tend to thrive on the emergence of a *dominating member,* and in this class discussion, not untypically, it is the teacher. He organizes the central themes of the discussion, moving it on, for example, from the things they know already to the questions they would like to ask. The children address all the remarks to him. He identifies, in most cases, the successive speakers. In terms of total number of contributions, he contributes the most. His dominance is complemented by the supportiveness and *solidarity* of the class. As every teacher knows, even a lecture, let alone a discussion, can fail to get anywhere because X is larking about, Y is displaying 'dumb insolence', Z is talking throughout in a very loud voice, and so on. Quite often, such behaviour seems less serious to the outside observer, and indeed to other pupils, as well as to X, Y or Z, than it does to the teacher - but this too is a part of the dynamics of the classroom situation (as it is of all social relationships.) One major consequence of this, is that 'difficult' classes have much more chance of achieving something in a group situation than as a single class, yet because they are difficult there is even less likelihood for the teacher feeling confident enough to let them work in groups at all. Indeed the setting up of groups is itself an act of confidence and trust on the teacher's part, and until group work becomes more 'everyday' in the classroom, teachers will very naturally continue to hold back from using small groups in the very situation where it is most valuable - where, as a single unit, the class is difficult, lacking in real solidarity and cohesiveness.

The Importance of Alternating between Class and Group Work

One important reason for alternating between class work and group work, in all contexts, but especially where the class presents the teacher with real social difficulties, is that the cohesion of a large group depends on the cohesion existing within the smaller groups of which it is made up. Hence the very real need for plenty of opportunities to work together in small units. Unfortunately, a lot of class discussions never become discussions at all;

there is so little solidarity that the impersonality of a good discussion can never be achieved, but must always give way to 'personality' - to the intrusion of personal friction and antagonism. Of course, such friction and antagonism can destroy many a potentially fruitful group discussion also, but the numerical odds in favour of this happening increase, logically, with the size of the group. And the personality of the teacher himself or herself, is a dynamic part of this process, itself creating friction and antagonism at certain times. Indeed the techniques adopted by the teacher to counter the difficulties of the classroom situation, can themselves become part of those difficulties.

A further good reason for alternating between group and class discussion, is that conventions can be 'tried out' in one for carrying over into the other. And this process can work in both directions. With this particular class discussion, for example, the teacher's use of questions in a fairly open-ended fashion can be seen as a model for the children to use with each other. The same applies to the even more fundamental convention of literally attending to all the points raised by all the children.

Deliberate Role-play and Impersonality

Deliberate role-play is more in evidence here. For example, the teacher at times professes genuine uncertainty, as at line 85, but mostly refuses to acknowledge what he actually knows. He feigns ignorance in order to encourage the pupils' contributions. He, as it were, says to the class - "I will say as little as possible, if you will say what you know", and the class join in this game very supportively. They also are remarkably good at taking their turn and waiting their turn. Only a couple of times are there interruptions of others' contributions. They also remain friendly, but cool - there are no tempers, no angry outbursts. Nobody cries out 'Rubbish!' or walks out in a huff.

It is worth adding that these criteria are also demonstrated by the teacher. He appears to listen to everyone; not to interrupt any one; and not to make anyone feel foolish for saying anything, nor even for saying nothing.

This type of cool impersonality is central to discussion. And indeed, discussion changes into debate once personality becomes a dominant theme. Then the aim is to defeat and to win, and this is accompanied by the sense of elation at winning and of dejection at losing. Discussion is, by contrast, detached. The discussion itself matters rather than the outcome; in effect, it is the pursuit of knowledge for its own sake. At its most sophisticated it is the symposium of like-minded specialists, all equipped with a broadly similar background and expertise, and hence able to take a great deal of knowledge (and attitudes) for granted in the cause of a discussion designed to extend further their knowledge or understanding. But the symposium disintegrates as soon as anybody starts winning. It is the shared internalizing of everybody's point of view, of the various riders and refinements and reservations, by all the participants, that distinguishes discussion (of which the symposium is the professional, highly specialized extreme example) from the debate, or the argument, or the friendly chat.

Thus, a discussion seeks to utilize the riders and reservations, to incorporate them into everybody else's thinking, where the debate seeks to destroy and obliterate them. Likewise, because discussion is impersonal it is also more friendly. No one is there to beat anybody else, hence there can be no insults, no abuse. Only the most sensitive and hyper-sensitive can be left feeling stupid. Hence, a part of the conventions is to accept literal errors, irrelevances and blunders in a cool enough and friendly enough fashion to keep everyone, including the blunderer, reasonably happy. Hence, as we have seen in the discussion on Cuba, Harry handles such encounters with a mixture of humour, jollying along, and what one could call 'diplomatic deafness' - which means that at certain times one either does not appear to hear precisely what has been said or alternatively, re-expresses it 'correctly' as if one has heard it that way in the first place. This is a basic part of keeping a dialogue alive.

At the same time, a discussion is not synonymous with a friendly chat, though friendly chats have a lot to commend them and have their own (important) place in learning and teaching. In a friendly chat what matters is the friendliness, and keeping the friendship going (or getting it started). Hence, in the course of a friendly chat we invariably give our assent to opinions we do not honestly share for, to do otherwise, would be to risk breaking the relationship, and establishing a distance instead of familiarity. In a discussion we do the opposite. The only sacrifices we make are those necessary to keep dialogue going, to leave our options open, and they are in the service of the ideas themselves, not of personalities.

Taking Turns

We have already stressed the importance of *taking turns,* but it is worth noting that this is infinitely more complex and strenuous in class than in group discussion - *if* one actually wishes to contribute. If one does not wish to contribute, then class discussion is infinitely less strenuous for one's silence is inconspicuous and insignificant. In other words, the very size of a class imposes limitations on the activity of the students. Because there are more of them than in a small group, so more of them have to spend more of the time saying nothing. This means not only that they have less chance to make significant contributions, but also that they have virtually no chance to engage in the very ordinary contributions, such as - 'Yeah' and 'Mm' - that conversation in small groups is littered with. And these 'Yeahs' and 'Mms' fulfil the major function of encouraging the speakers while also affirming the involvement of the listeners. Indeed, it could be fairly argued that it is harder to listen in any real sense in a large group than in a small group, for the simple reason that the listener is not kept alert by the opportunity and even the need to articulate his or her understanding. In this way it could be further argued that a student who listens to what a friend is saying in a group, actually has a greater chance of extending his knowledge, than the same student listening to the teacher in class, and this is quite separate from whether or not the student uses the occasion actively to question and to work things out for himself. The longer one has to remain silent (not to mention still or static) the harder it is to concentrate and hence to listen.

Hence, the conventional demands of a class discussion are greater in certain respects than those of a group discussion.

Changing the Conventions

In both types of discussion, *development and experiment* are possible. The teacher can, for example, ask the class to make notes during the discussion; to look at whoever happens to be speaking; or to present opinions in the form of questions. Similarly teachers can, and should, experiment with their own roles, at times, for instance, saying nothing; at times playing the devil's advocate; at times remaining resolutely detached. As an example, Lawrence Stenhouse has argued that for a really valid discussion to take place on any moral issue (valid in the sense of itself contributing to the students' moral development) the teacher must act as an entirely impartial chairman, and not himself, or herself, contribute an opinion or judgement. This is a form of change, or experiment, in the conventions of discussion which students undoubtedly find stimulating at certain times and can indeed give them a technique for themselves to use elsewhere. At the same time it could become self-defeating, even in the limited context of class discussion of moral issues, if the teacher employs it always.

Equally useful is for the teacher not to 'take the chair' at all, but to sit among the class, perhaps at some times inviting someone else to take the chair (with the single function of identifying the person who is to speak next) and at other times operating without any such 'chairperson'.

Whatever the teacher does, he or she has to remember that his or her behaviour is itself a primary model for the behaviour of the students. It is not the only model, of course, but it is nevertheless a very significant one. Teachers who look at the person speaking and actually appear to listen; who can remain silent for whole lengths of time without appearing to lose interest; who can enjoy disagreement with their own observations; who can maintain a cool friendliness - such teachers are literally teaching their students the conventions of good discussion and, less directly, encouraging good thinking.

Ways of Thinking

What characterizes the ways in which the class think as they engage in this discussion?

Missed Opportunities

Class discussion, like group discussion, tends to contain various *missed opportunities* - those occasional, but golden moments and asides, flashes of insight and understanding, which are unnoticed and unexplored. Often this is not because of anyone's laziness, but again because of the particular sense of relevance which is guiding the discussion, such that interesting possibilities are dismissed prematurely. Also, where teachers are themselves nervous and insecure (as when they are being observed by their superiors) they may hold on so tightly to what they think is relevant that virtually everything the class offers threatens to be massively irrelevant. Mere pressures of time, and a feeling that we must 'get through' the discussion before the bell goes, can be equally fatal.

The teacher on this occasion seems deliberately to miss a large number of opportunities to correct children's errors. His aim is that the children should have the chance to air what they know, what they do not know, and what they misunderstand. (He thus runs the risk, it is worth noting, of being criticized for allowing children to mislead other children.) The underlying principle on which the teacher works is that all the material of this lesson will be taken up later. One of his tasks, then, is to ensure that he knows subsequently what has been said - whether by taking notes during, or immediately after, the lesson.

Precision: Creativity

The teacher's technique in this discussion seems to help at least some of the children to express their ideas in very *precise* and also *economic* terms. Bill at line 39; Bill again at line 71; Vince at line 78, and again at line 86: these are instances of children thinking out their ideas very carefully and explicitly, very much under the active encouragement of the teacher, and with the whole class having the chance to internalize what is going on.

Many of the points made are very much thought out by the children in their own terms, and not simply recapitulated versions of what they have heard or read. For example, Vince's explanation of the demise of the herbivores is given not once, but twice, the second time in a different form. These are quite creative contributions. Similarly, in many of their questions there is a genuine attempt to bring together different areas of their experience, to form *new wholes* from different *parts*. There is for instance, Winston's question at line 104:

I don't understand - Why didn't one of the dinosaurs live longer than the rest? Why didn't he live on the rest?

It is the kind of question which many adults, and most teachers, are tempted to answer on the spot, briskly and efficiently. In fact, it is ideal material for group discussion with the boy's peers, for they are far more likely to move around the topic, and, more important, make it possible for the boy to continue to spell out his difficulties until he feels they are resolved.

Inequality of Effort

All discussion is characterized by a certain *inequality of effort.* Not everyone will try equally hard, and some will appear to try, or to think, very little. Note that this is not the same as saying very little. It is perfectly possible for the person who says the least to think the most, and to go away from the discussion greatly enriched and stimulated. Likewise, it is perfectly possible for someone who says a very great deal to have very little to offer and to expend the minimum of effort in offering it.

No amount of 'clever' teaching circumvents this phenomenon. All the teacher can do is to vary his techniques, along some such lines as we have already indicated, and thus in effect give the students different contexts in which to try again. The problem is endemic in all activity, and in all teaching, not only in class or group discussion. It occurs in *all* other class activities including reading and writing. The child who is untouched by a good class discussion may also be untouched by the most fascinating of books and may even have been untouched, given the chance, by the act of creating the universe in seven days and seven nights.

Indeed the child, like the adult, has that basic and inalienable option. Too often though, class (and group) discussions are judged as ineffectual simply because some of the class or group seem uninvolved and unimpressed. A teacher needs to note the fact and to seek to vary his techniques another time with a view to involving these children or these students in particular, but the problem itself is not peculiar to discussion, nor is it a criticism of its effectiveness.

In the class discussion on the beginnings of life on earth, it is worth noting that in the 10 minutes or so covered by this particular extract, roughly half the class actually say something - 13 out of 25. Of these, at least some of the children appear to be thinking out their ideas and not simply recapitulating them. This is especially so in relation to Bill's explanation of fossils (line 40) and Vince's explanation of the demise of dinosaurs (line 80). Similarly, the questions at the end seem to express very genuine doubts and an accompanying desire to learn.

The Knowledge Used

By inviting the children to express what they already know, the teacher is able to 'tune in' to many of the *assumptions,* including the false assumptions, that they are making. In a slightly different way, Niresh's question at line 103 is a good example of the dangers of a teacher assuming that everyone has heard or understood something that has already been quite fully explained (at line 73 onwards). Also, the invitation encourages the children to make links with a variety of knowledge and experience in a way that a more highly structured session might not do. They talk about dinosaurs, Tollund Man, archaeology, amphibians, fossils, the ice-age and how life started. Their sense of what is *relevant* is kept usefully wide.

The Language Used

Class discussion creates the opportunity for children to internalize the language of the teacher. On this occasion the teacher is engaged not in criticizing or even analyzing, but in supporting and encouraging. To be precise, he does three different things. He invites questions: 'Any ideas? . . . Any questions? . . . Anybody like to add to that?'. Secondly, he expresses support and enthusiasm: 'Very interesting . . . very good . . . marvellous!'. And thirdly, he asks people to rearticulate some of the points they make: 'Can you explain that again?', 'Can you just take us through that again?'. He thus offers the children a viable model of parts of the language, parts of the register, of discussion. They thus have the chance of learning such a language for themselves.

Group Discussion and Class Discussion: A Comparison

Both kinds of discussion merit a major place in the school curriculum. But neither kind is widely employed. Group discussion is viewed mostly with suspicion, and class discussion is often closer to a lecture by the teacher than to a discussion by the whole class. Lectures have a useful role to play, but it is a very different role.

Class discussion is in one sense, as we have already indicated, more difficult to achieve because of the inevitable hierarchical difference between teachers and pupils or students. Such a difficulty is therefore not unique to the classroom. It occurs wherever there is a hierarchy. For example, employers and employees; officers and men; professors and research assistants; leading actors and assistant stage-managers: these and countless other hierarchical relationships render real discussion difficult. The reason is, of course, that the hierarchy itself rests on certain conventions that cut across the dispassionate objectively of a good discussion. At its most elementary, this may mean that X must always have either the last word, or the most decisive word. It may even mean that nobody else's word is much worth listening to (and students who believe this will therefore declare that they learn nothing from discussing problems with each other.) Readers of Thomas Kuhn's *The Structure of Scientific Revolutions* will be familiar with countless other ways in which hierarchies inhibit thought. But, even so, a great deal of very good discussion does take place within hierarchical institutions, including schools and colleges. But an effort, as it were, is needed to overcome the basic hierarchical limitations. Some such efforts will misfire, and sometimes such efforts work more effectively in the minds of the superiors who inaugurate them than they do in the minds of those further down the ladder. Countless movies and novels have illustrated the comic follies of invitations to 'Call me by my first name, George' and the subsequent confusion (intellectual as well as social) that this can cause.

Not the least virtue of group discussion is that it enables pupils to play the role of the teacher, just as Harry does in the group discussion on Cuba. One could say that the problem for the teacher is to create situations where Harry can play the teacher, and then Philip, and then Andrew, and then Vince, and then everybody else. It is by such means that the greatest opportunities for language development are to be found.

Summary: The Teacher's Role in Group and Class Discussions

1. The two activities are in no way mutually exclusive. There is a real need for classes to engage in group and in class discussion, for each will in various ways create a model to influence the other. The teacher has an important part to play in both.

2. The teacher has to find ways of teaching children how to discuss things together, whether as a class or as a small group. Sometimes this is done by talking about the kinds of approaches that are useful; sometimes it is done by the teacher joining in and illustrating them; sometimes it is done by changing the ways in which the group is working.

3. Class and group discussions always contain some missed opportunities, and it is very uncommon for all the participants to contribute equally. In general, there is more likelihood of people contributing in smaller groups than in larger ones, and even their span of attention is likely to be greater in smaller groups.

4. Class and group discussions offer important opportunities for children to explore a range of knowledge; to make links between the familiar and the unfamiliar; to ask their own questions, and to think things out. The teacher's contribution towards these will lie, first, in the sessions leading up to the discussion, as the groundwork is laid for children to extend their experience through reading, listening, talking and writing. Secondly, the teacher is influential as a member of the class or as a member of a group. His or her attentiveness, types of questions, attitude and change of at-

titude (as when the teacher changes from partiality to impartiality) all have an effect on the children's sense of what is and what is not a discussion.

5. Discussing different things, for different purposes, with different people, is an important part of language development.

5

Reading:
Group Discussion of a Passage

Introduction

We have looked so far at the process of talking in a context of people discussing issues and problems where they have to some extent already assimilated the evidence that they are handling. Equally important is the activity of talking about what we are reading, of using the opportunities of raising questions with one another in order to begin to make sense together of what initially may seem difficult or deceptively easy. It is not unfair to suggest that traditionally in our schools we have related reading to writing but seldom related it to talking.

Talking about what we read is one way of seeking to understand it. It is also, therefore, a way of teaching reading, not least because it can help to highlight the difficulties of the reader.

These difficulties can be of four main kinds:

1. *Difficulty of Subject-matter*

At any stage in our lives, no matter how extensive our education, we can be defeated by a text simply because its subject-matter is too unfamiliar. We can build no bridges between it and ourselves.

2. *Complexity of Thinking*

In various ways, a text can be difficult to come to terms with because of the kind of thinking which it represents. For example, massive precision and massive economy, employed together, make equally massive demands on the reader. Many official law reports, for instance, such as those published in *The Times* are hard reading even for practising lawyers. But likewise a highly imprecise piece of writing is a tough proposition for the reader, who then has to perform a major surgical operation on the text before it can become simple sense to him. The same is true of a text that is totally lacking in economy, that repeats itself and elaborates and takes a lot of time establishing what the reader suspects has already been established. Also, in many cases, a highly creative piece of writing may be so original as to be very challenging indeed to the reader. Such complexity is always a two-way process. What is difficult for one reader is highly accessible to another.

3. *Complexity of Language*

Broadly speaking, langauge becomes more daunting when its units become longer. In general, longer words, longer sentences, longer paragraphs, longer essays, longer books are more difficult than short ones. Hence the reader's familiarity with these longer units of utterance is an important factor in the task. Also important is the reader's familiarity with the particular register in which the text is written. Even someone who has followed with interest an experiment in a chemistry laboratory, may be defeated by a text-book report of the experiment if such reporting is unfamiliar to him. Similarly, the absence of extra-lingusitic aids, such as illustrations, headings and sub-headings, large print and generous spacing can become a factor in the reader's difficulties, until he becomes used to their absence.

4. *Ways of Working*

Finally, the particular ways in which the reader organizes his or her work on a text, may itself relate to the difficulties of reading it. For example, a reader can be helped by putting a text aside to come back to it later, by talking about a text before reading it. (What is it about? Does it answer any kind of question? What do I expect from it?), and by talking about what is being read with a peer group. It is this latter device which we wish to look at in this chapter.

Group Discussion of a Text

Here are a group of *11-year-olds* discussing a passage in a science lesson. Their brief has been to (a) read the passage through, (b) talk about anything they find difficult or do not feel sure about and, (c) see if they can agree on the two or three main points made in the passage.

The passage itself has a reading difficulty of about 51 on the Flesch scoring method, which means that it demands a reading age of about 16 or 17. The children in this group are roughly average for their age. When they were tested by their school, a month or so previously, their scores on the Widespan Reading Test were as follows: Albert (a reading age of 12); Subash (11); Gajendran (9); and Steven (11).

We begin with the passage itself, and follow this with their taped discussion.

THE INTERNAL TEMPERATURE OF THE SUN

The surface of the sun is continually losing heat to outer-space and at a great rate too, yet the surface of the temperature remains constant. Clearly, the surface must be gaining heat from the interior as fast as it loses it to space, and it follows that the interior must be hotter than the surface. Since the Sun's surface is already hot enough to vaporize all known substances, and since the interior of the Sun is hotter still, it seems reasonable to suppose that the Sun is gaseous in nature, - just a globe of super-hot gas. If this is so, then astronomers are fortunate, for the qualities of gases are easier to understand than are the qualities of liquids and solids.

The English astronomer, Arthur Eddington (1882 - 1944) argued that if the Sun were affected only by its own gravitational force, then it would collapse. The fact that it did not collapse meant that some force was working against gravity, and this force was working in the opposite direction from gravity (from within, outwards). He then argued that this force could be produced by the expansive tendencies of gases at high temperatures.

Taking into account the mass of the Sun and the strength of its gravitational force, Eddington calculated the temperatures required to balance the Sun's surface and ended up with amazing figures. The temperature at the Sun's centre reached the colossal figure of 15 000 000 degrees centigrade. (Recent calculations put this figure almost half as high again.)

Eddington's argument helps to explain something else. The Sun, he said, was in a state of delicate balance between gravitational force pulling inwards and the colossal temperature pushing outwards. But what if some other stars were not? Suppose instead, that a particular star was not quite hot enough to oppose the force of its own gravity? Such a star would collapse inwards, but eventually, as it did so, its own heat would increase. As the heat increased, the star would expand again, only to collapse again, and so to start the whole cycle all over again. Such a star would regularly 'pulsate' - and hence the term 'pulsar'. Such stars are indeed to be seen in the sky, and Eddington's argument seems to explain them.

The Group Discussion

Gajendran: *We'll talk about the main points first.*
Subash: *We'll read it first.*
Albert: *Yeah. Read it first.*

Subash:	*Let Steven go first. Go that way.*	
Albert:	*Read it properly, paragraph at a time. And discuss it.*	(5)
Subash:	*First paragraph.*	

(Steven reads the first paragraph aloud, without any apparent difficulty.)

Gadendran:	*Now do you understand it?*	
Albert:	*Do a bit at a time.*	
Subash:	*Steven, what does* constant *mean?*	(10)
Steven:	*Constant means - it's the same all the time.*	
Albert:	*Yeah, that's right.*	
Subash:	*You sure about it?*	
Albert:	(Re-reads the first sentence.) *That means: the surface of the sun - all the heat's that coming out of it, is going into outer-space.*	(15)
Gajendran:	*Yeah, and it's wasted. Goes away.*	
Subash:	*What does* interior *mean, anyone?*	
Gajendran:	*The inside of the sun.*	
Subash:	*Not the inside of the sun. Anything.*	(20)
Albert:	*Now what does this one mean?*	
Subash:	*Which one?*	
Albert:	(Re-reads the second sentence.)	
Gajendran:	*It means . . .*	
Albert:	*All the heat from the interior is going through the sun and going out.*	(25)
Subash:	*Next paragraph.*	
Albert:	*No, wait. Wait. 'and it follows that the interior must be hotter than the surface.' That means - that inside it's got to be hotter because . . .*	(30)
Subash:	*There's more gas.*	
Albert:	*That's where all the energy comes from.*	
Subash:	*Now who's gonna read the second paragraph?*	

(Albert reads the second paragraph aloud, again without difficulty.)

Subash:	*Right. Steven, what's your question now? What do you think?*	(35)
Gajendran:	*It means that . . .*	
Subash:	*Let him talk.*	
Steven:	*It means that . . . 'The qualities of gases are easier to understand than the qualities of liquids and solids.'*	(40)
Albert:	*So it means that the gases that are in the sun are easier to understand than the liquids and solids that are on earth.*	
Subash:	*Yes. Now, what's* vaporize *anyone?*	
Gajendran:	*When a thing comes up to each other, it kind of*	(45)

disintegrates, kind of disappears, you know. Melting or
something into thin air.

Subash: *Mm.*

Albert: *What does this mean - 'It seems reasonable to suppose*
             that the sun is gaseous in nature.'?   (50)

Gajendran: *That means . . .*

Subash: *Now listen. Steven ain't having a say.*

Steven: *Oh!*

Subash: *Come on. You've got to have a say.*

Steven: *Can I ask another question then?*   (55)

Subash: *Yes, go on. Ask another question.*

Steven: *What is - 'just a globe of super-hot gas'?*

Subash: *Think about it . . . Don't you know?*

Steven: *No.*

Subash: *A globe of super-hot gas is just a globe, like the earth* (60)
             is a globe. And it's super-hot gas.

(Subash reads the third paragraph, and stops at the end of the
first sentence.)

Subash: *Now, I'll stop there right? And we'll gather up on that*
             sentence.   (65)

Albert: *That means - that - the amount of gravity in the sun . . .*
             You see, I think . . .

Subash: *That the sun would collapse if it was affected by its own*
             gravity.

Albert: *It would turn into a black hole.*   (70)

Subash: *No. It would just come down. It would collapse. Cause*
             it isn't strong enough.

Gajendran: *Kind of grow smaller.*

Steven: *It would just go inwards.*

Gajendran: *Go into a white dwarf or something.*   (75)

(Subash continues reading the third paragraph, stopping this time at
the end of the second sentence.)

Subash: *Now, Steven, what do you think of that? You aren't*
             listening, are you?

Gajendran: *He is listening, but he doesn't understand most of it,*   (80)
             I think.

Subash: *Do you want me to read it a bit slower?*

Others: *Yeah.*

(Subash rereads the sentence.)

Subash: *What do you think of that? Don't you know?*   (85)

Steven: *Not quite . . . 'The fact that it did not collapse . . .'*

	No!	
Subash:	*Let Gajendran have a go.*	
Gajendran:	*No. I want to ask a question first.*	
Subash:	*All right.*	(90)
Gajendran:	*Why . . . mm . . . why does it have to collapse? Cause I don't understand the bit where . . .*	
Subash:	*Well, the sun ain't affected by its own gravity, is it. But if it was affected, it would go inwards.*	
Gajendran:	*Oh, yes.*	(95)
Subash:	*But it isn't yet . . .*	

(Gajendran now starts to read the fourth paragraph.)

Subash:	*I haven't finished my sentence yet. Now you know that last bit. have we all got it?*	
Gajendran:	*No one's got what it means.*	(100)
Albert:	*That means there was a sort of force . . .*	
Subash:	*Something was kind of holding it from gravity - which was fighting against gravity to hold it up.*	
Albert:	*The force inside the core that was coming out . . .*	
Subash:	*Was holding it against the fire with the gravity. Was holding the sun up.*	(105)

(Subash now reads the last sentence of the third paragraph.)

Subash;	*What does* tendencies *mean, Gajendran?*	
Gajendran:	*The reaction of the gases. What they can do, you know. Blow up or something.*	(110)
Steven:	Expansive - *big, getting bigger.*	
Albert:	*It says here - that the force that was keeping the sun like as it was, is quite a lot of gases at really high temperatures. That kept all the force. That kept the sun as it was.*	(115)
Steven:	*But we ain't getting to the* expansive tendencies.	
Subash:	*Yes. That's it. That's the main point. Expansive is the big tendencies.*	
Gajendran:	*Where it goes bigger.*	
Subash:	*Tendencies of gases getting bigger, and getting hotter.*	(120)
Gajendran:	*The gas is getting . . .*	
Subash:	*Very hot. Do you understand that, Steven?*	
Gajendran:	*At the surface of the sun, right . . .*	
Subash:	*It's getting bigger.*	
Gajendran:	*It's slowly getting bigger and bigger, and the gases are getting hotter. You understand it now?*	(125)
Steven:	*Yeah.*	

Subash:	*The sun's getting bigger and bigger, and the gases are getting hotter. You got any more questions?*

(Gajendran starts to read paragraph four.) (130)

Subash:	(Stopping him at the end of the first sentence) *Leave it there.*
Gajendran:	*Who understands it?*
Albert:	*We've got to discuss it.*
Subash:	*Okay. Right. Look -* 'Taking into account the mass of (135) the sun . . .' *That is: remembering the weight of it.* '. . . and the strength of its gravitational force . . .' *that's what's pulling it, the strength of gravity.*
Albert:	*It's pulling all the planets.*
Steven:	*It's keeping all the planets into orbit.* (140)
Albert:	*Yeah.*
Subash:	*That's gravity, isn't it. Keeping it in orbit. Pulling it down into orbit.* (He rereads the first sentence of the fourth paragraph.) *What does this mean?*
Gajendran:	*What he means is - em: how much gravity is needed -* (145) *against the different depths of the sun - like down at the core, half-way up, three-quarters up or three-quarters down.*
Subash:	*That doesn't need explaining much, He's done it. You go on, Gajendran.* (150)

(Gajendran reads the second sentence of the fourth paragraph.)

Subash:	*Who understands that?*
Albert:	*That means . . .*
Subash:	Colossal *means massive.*
Albert:	*The temperature in the core . . .* (155)
Gajendran:	*It means the real, the amazing, the real temperature of the sun in the core is about 15 million degrees centigrade.*
Subash:	*That is the interior, inside. Right?*
Steven:	*Yeah, that's it.*
Albert:	*'Recent calculations . . .' What does that mean?* (160)
Subash:	*'Recent calculations . . .' that is, not very long ago.* '. . . *put this figure . . .' that is . . .*
Gajendran:	*The latest figure has been higher.*

(Steven reads the first half of the last paragraph.
Subash then starts going through it again.) (165)

Subash:	Delicate balance - *that is in a . . . moving easily.*
Gajendran:	*I don't understand it still.*
Subash;	*You know what* delicate *means, don't you. Very . . .*

Albert:	*Fragile.*	
Subash:	*Yeah, fragile. And it will move . . .*	(170)
Albert:	*And it would probably collapse.*	
Subash:	*'. . . between the gravitational force pulling inwards . . .'*	
Albert:	*Gravitation's going inwards.*	
Subash:	*'. . . and the colossal temperature pushing outwards.'*	
	That's the heat. - Steven, stop doing that!	(175)
Gajendran:	*Steven, do you understand it or not?*	
Albert:	*What does he mean by, - 'But what if some other stars were not . . .?' Steven?*	
Subash:	*He's not listening. Let me say it. If other stars weren't resisting - you know, to gravity - then they would just collapse.*	(180)

(Albert reads the remainder of the last paragraph, stopping at the end of the sentence - 'such a star would collapse inwards. . .')

Subash:	*Gajendran, you do that.*	
Gajendran:	*It means, I think, that a particular star, one star, a particular star, if it wasn't hot enough . . . to resist - er - resist. . . .*	(185)
Albert:	*No. If the star wasn't strong enough to resist gravity, it would just collapse inwards.*	
Gajendran:	*Oh, resist its own gravity!*	(190)
Albert:	*Yeah, that's it.*	
Subash:	*Yeah, that's it. You go on now, Albert.*	

(Albert rereads the sentence beginning - 'such a star. . . .' and moves on to the following sentence.)

Subash:	*This is getting complicated. Now Steven, you're not doing anything.*	(195)
Gajendran:	*Steven, please!*	
Subash:	*Tell all you know, right?*	
Steven:	*What, ask a question?*	
Gajendran:	*You're not going to get anywhere.*	(200)
Subash:	*Let him think for a couple of minutes. . . You don't know, do you Steven?*	
Steven:	*'Such a star would collapse inwards, but eventually, as it did so, its own heat would increase.'*	
Albert:	*Yes, what does that mean? How come the heat would increase as it collapsed? Cause it would be dying, running out of energy.*	(205)
Subash:	*It will increase cause the inside thing will come out, won't it. The inside, the interior, will just come out.*	

Gajendran:	*All the gases and so on will kind of go larger and go* (210) *hotter, and the more heat they give the more larger the sun would grow.*
Albert:	*No, listen.*
Subash:	*No. That's not the point. Go on, Albert.*
Albert:	*Whan a star collapses, all the heat that was inside and* (215) *didn't escape, comes out and expands it. But as soon as the star meets with gravity, it's too strong for it, and it collapses in again. And it comes back out again and collapses again. Keeps doing that.*
Subash:	*I'm trying to say - is - the heat inside will come out when* (220) *it collapses, won't it.*
Albert:	*Yeah.*
Subash:	*It won't stay in, will it. Has to come out. That's why it's so hot.*
Albert:	*If it turns into a black hole, the heat will just go* (225) *through, won't it.*

(Bell goes for end of lesson.)

Subash:	*Now listen. Do you want to . . . do you want to read the whole of it? Cause we know all this now. We don't know it, but we've got an idea what it is. So next time,* (230) *we'll work out our main points.*

Commentary on the Discussion: Their Thinking

A number of interesting things are happening. One of the striking aspects of the contributions of all four children is their willingness to say what puzzles them. They all ask questions of each other.

Asking Questions

At one point, for example, instead of answering someone else's question, as he is expected to do, Steven asks a question of his own (line 55), and Gajendran does the same thing at line 89. Both of them insist that they do not understand something, even when someone else appears to have explained it, as when Steven says, 'But we ain't getting to the expansive tendencies' (line 116) and when Gajendran says, 'I don't understand it still' (line 167). Albert asks fewer questions, but like Subash, who asks most, it is not always clear whether he is asking them because he wants to clarify a difficulty or to test the others (and thus keep the discussion going). Nevertheless, they are very clearly moving towards learning by questioning, and at one point, when Steven is urged to tell all he knows, he replies, 'What, ask a question?' (line 199).

Taking Time

Allied to this is an insistence at certain times that the discussion should not be rushed forward with doubts still lingering. They are prepared to *make each other wait*. Thus Albert stops Subash from moving too quickly through the first paragraph (line 28). Similarly, Subash later stops Gajendran (line 98), and at a number of points stops the readers from moving on in order to initiate talk about each sentence in turn.

In this way, there is a fair amount of *disputing and refining* of ideas in order to achieve a better understanding of the text. One of the best moments is when Gajendran simply says, 'No one's got what it means' (line 100) in reply to Subash's, 'Have we all got it?'. And a little later, when Gajendran asks, 'Who understands it?' (line 133), Albert replies, 'We've got to discuss it' (line 134). It is also Albert who clarifies Gajendran's paraphrase of the behaviour of pulsars, by simply saying, 'No' (line 188) and then offering a more pithy explanation of his own: 'If the star wasn't strong enough to resist gravity, it would just collapse inwards'. And a little later, he again corrects Gajendran's explanation of the same thing, and is supported here by Subash - 'No, listen' and, 'That's not the point. Go on, Albert' (line 214). In fact, it is only Steven who does not get around to putting this point (perhaps the central point in the whole passage) into his own words, though it is Albert who does so the most succinctly and who also develops it into a further point of his own, relating the idea of a pulsar to that of a black hole (line 225).

Meanings of Words

They give a lot of care to the meanings of words, discussing, for example, *constant, interior, vaporize, tendencies, expansive, colossal* and *delicate*. They are at times almost pedantic in their keenness to get things right, as when Subash corrects Gajendran for defining 'interior' as the inside of the sun and insists that it means the inside of anything (line 20). There are also times when they do not simply pull down their definitions from memory, as it were, but can be heard working them out, as when Gajendran goes through concepts such as disintegrating and disappearing before coming up with, 'melting or something into thin air', when seeking to define 'vaporize' (line 45). Gajendran is equally adventurous when wrestling with a concept very difficult to pin down, namely, 'tendencies' (line 108). Similarly, Subash and Albert together have a brave shot at explaining to Gajendran the meaning of a 'delicate balance' (line 170). It is important, too, that they at all times, having defined the words, then reread the whole sentence together and so in effect put their definitions to the test.

The Limitations of Their Thinking: Lack of Precision

Inevitably, there are also points in the discussion where they do not think hard enough. They are sometimes, as we have seen, very precise indeed. But a degree of imprecision runs right through their talking. One of the best moments in the discussion is when Gajendran asks: '. . . why does it (the Sun) have to collapse?' (line 91). According to the passage, it was Eddington's belief that, if the Sun were affected *only* by its own gravity, then collapse would be inevitable. The reason for this belief is not really spelt out in the passage, but is nevertheless central to it. It is a pity that Subash's reply paraphrases the text rather than probes the justification for this assertion. Gajendran however, accepts the reply at that particular point and they then move on - or rather they begin to do so. But almost immediately Subash returns to the same point: 'Now you know that last bit. Have we all got it?' (line 99), and it is then that Gajendran affirms, 'No one's got what it means'. Albert now begins an explanation, but is twice taken over by Subash whose thinking is confused and confusing, suggesting that something 'was holding the sun up' (line 106). They now again move on to other things, but because the point is so central to the whole passage, they inevitably come back to it. Albert now makes a fuller attempt to explain his own interpretation (line 112) which is to some extent misinterpreted by both Gajendran and Subash in the conviction that they have got it right (lines 125 and 128).

The point recurs in their discussion of the last few sentences. This time, Subash does a rather better job of clarifying the point: 'If other stars weren't resisting - you know, to gravity - then they would just collapse' (line 180) and Gajendran appears to start spelling out the same idea for himself. Albert now insists that this is wrong, and says simply, 'If the star wasn't strong enough to resist gravity, it would just collapse inwards' (line 189). Gajendran then assimilates this to his own line of thinking, and says, 'Oh, resist its own gravity!'.

They are back at the same point almost immediately when Steven, under pressure to make a useful contribution, reads out the same sentence which they have just been analyzing: 'Such a star would collapse inwards, but eventually, as it did so, its own heat would increase'. Far from wasting the time of the others, this proves a most useful lead for their own thinking. Albert rephrases the sentence by turning it into a very helpful question: 'How come the heat would increase as it collapsed? Cause it would be dying, running out of energy' (line 207). Subash and Gajendran (but not Steven) now have a go at answering the question in terms of the inner heat of the sun causing its expansion. It is only Albert who is able to bring together the two ideas of the expanding tendency of hot gas and the contracting tendency of gravity to explain the pulsations of such stars, and, when time runs out, none of the others has taken his explanation and re-expressed it in his own words, even though all of them appear to have assented to it as a fair account of the point made in the passage.

There are a number of other points in the discussion where they do not *push themselves or each other to find their own words,* their own language, for the things they find difficult. Steven is not urged to put the definition of a 'globe of super-hot gas' into the context of the passage (line 57); and a little later he is asked if he understands the point about the expansive tendencies, but again he is not asked to find his own words to express himself (line 126). The same is true when Gajendran inquires about 'delicate balance' (line 166). He is given answers, but that is that.

Likewise, at several points they *do not pursue errors* made by each other, even where they are probably aware that an error has been made. The most significant example of this is when Subash incorrectly paraphrases the first sentence of the third paragraph to read, '. . . the sun would collapse if it was affected by its own gravity' (line 69). In fact, in the passage itself, the writer states - 'Eddington argued that if the Sun were affected *only* by its own gravitational force, then it would collapse.' Subash thus overlooks the key word - *only*, and there is some evidence that he spends the rest of the discussion thinking that gravity is not part of the problem. But Albert is well aware of the correct reading of the passage, and yet does not directly draw his attention to this. Similarly, Subash later talks of the sun being pulled by gravity (line 138) where he again seems to have misunderstood the passage, and he is himself then misunderstood by both Albert and Steven, for they then go on to talk about the gravitational pull that keeps the planets in orbit. None of them stops the others to ask, What is gravity? What kinds of gravity are there? What particular kind is being talked about here?

Knowledge Used

They deploy a range of relevant knowledge about the behaviour of the stars and planets, demonstrating some understanding of concepts such as gravity, black holes, and the movement of the heavenly bodies, but they tend not to argue when the things they think they know are contradicted by others. Thus, Albert makes the very plausible suggestion that a star, affected only by its own gravity, would turn into a black hole (line 70) but does not reply to Subash's contradictory comment - 'No. It would just come down'. Similarly, they do not have a consistent policy of questioning the use of concepts which they either do not themselves know (as, probably, with Gajendran's reference to the white dwarf, line 75) or which are used confusingly, and probably incorrectly, as when Subash jumps from the idea of the planets moving in orbit to that of the sun moving in orbit (line 142). Nobody takes him up to this. But most centrally, it is again the concept of gravity which trips them up. They assume too readily that they all know enough about it. They need to explore it, to ask questions about it, to seek further guidance about it.

Ways of Working
They work together very well, under the dominance of one of their members, but they all support him and help to keep the discussion alive.

Dominating Member, Supported by the Others
Subash takes charge of the proceedings from the very beginning, and all the others in various ways support him and help to keep the discussion going under his leadership. Gajendran begins by saying, 'We'll talk about the main points first', but Subash at once corrects him by insisting, 'We'll read it first.' And this is precisely what they do. Subash then organizes the reading of the passage, with each of them taking a paragraph in turn. He also initiates most of the questions, and repeatedly halts the readings so that they can explore specific details.

Not only do the others support him, but they also adopt some of his own techniques, such that Steven is at various points cajoled by all of the other three into making a more meaningful contribution to the session. This feeling that they are all responsible for the success of the activity under Subash's leadership also makes for a remarkable degree of mutual tolerance and support. People are not only allowed to speak, but positively encouraged to do so. Contributions are at times critized, but are never laughed at or shouted down. Declarations of ignorance or incomprehension are met, not with abuse, but with genuine attempts to assist and explain. And there are likewise moments when there is a real collective sense of coping with something that is tough - as when Subash breaks off from Albert's reading of the last paragraph to explain, 'This is getting complicated' (line 195).

Limitations
Inevitably, the discussion also illustrates the limitations of their way of working. For example, Subash has internalized a fairly autocratic model of discussion in which he becomes an ultimate authority on all the matters that are raised. He never asks a question to which he does not himself think he knows the answer. Indeed, there are moments when he shows the strain of carrying so much authority on his shoulders. An important point where this occurs is when Gajendran is very probably raising the whole business of the sun's gravity, and Subash states: 'Well, the sun ain't affected by its own gravity, is it' (line 93). It is made not as a tentative suggestion, or as a question, but as a simple statement. Nor does Subash hold his fire while asking others for their suggestions. There seems little doubt that in this way, the model they follow in their discussion, while opening up a number of fruitful possibilities, also very much confines them.

This same model also seems to make all three of them very concerned that Steven should do more than he actually does. He is asked to ask questions, and asked to suggest answers, and asked what he is thinking, and at one point he is asked by Subash to 'stop doing that!' and told by Gajendran - 'You're not going to get anywhere' (line 200). In fact though, Steven does not do at all badly. He several times says what he does not understand, once offers a definition that is not solicited by anyone else (line 111), and does not at any point appear to set out to destroy the discussion or demoralize any of his colleagues. But he does not initiate any of the questions, nor does he really attempt to re-articulate any of the points made in his own language. Hence it is never clear whether he is learning anything or not, and this manifestly irritates Subash and, to a lesser degree, Gajendran. Whether their technique for handling the problem is very effective is questionable, but what is interesting and impressive is that they do have a go at handling it and their attempt to do so does not seem to weaken their own zest for the discussion.

Language Used

It is interesting that the children seem to cope remarkably well, in many respects, with a passage that linguistically, at least, ought to be too difficult for them. As we said earlier, the passage appears to demand a reading age of 16 or 17, and yet the children are themselves only 11, and their reading ages are roughly the same as their chronological age.

A good example of this, is Gajendran's willingness to wrestle with the meaning of 'vaporize', at line 44. He comes up with 'disappears', and also 'disintegrates' before settling for 'melting into thin air'. He is similarly adventurous when faced with the question, what does 'tendencies' mean? He explains it as 'The reaction of the gases. What they can do,' (line 109). For a boy with an alleged reading age of 9 this is surprisingly good. And the same is true of the others. Albert's reading age is slightly higher than the others (his is 12), but, even so, it is quite impressive that he can comprehend so clearly the main point made in the passage - as when he explains the point several times to the others, at line 215 and subsequently. Subash and Steven have reading ages of 11, but again it is impressive that they have such an interest in the language of the passage and willingness to pursue its meaning.

The difficulties they encounter are not unto themselves difficulties with the language. It is not that the words are too long, or the style too elusive, or the grammatical structures too complicated. Their major difficulty lies in their familiarity (or lack of it) with certain key issues in astronomy, such as gravity, and a tendency to jump too readily from the parts of the passage to the whole. This happens, for instance, in Subash's omission of the word 'only' from the sentence that causes them so much trouble.

In other words, there is a very real case for encouraging children, right across the curriculum, to read material together which, on a purely linguistic level, is perhaps too advanced for them. Perhaps too, this is one way in which their reading, individually, can make progress. Certainly it would seem to be a mistake to base a syllabus on texts that are comfortably within their present 'reading scores'.

The Teacher's Role

Obviously the teacher's role in a reading session such as this is essentially the same as we have already outlined in relation to the teaching of discussion. In various ways the teacher encourages children to extend the ways in which they work, the kinds of knowledge on which they draw, the qualities of their thinking and the language they use. But a couple of points can be made briefly in relation to this specific group discussion. First, it illustrates very clearly the children's need for *more models* on which to draw in their thinking of how to conduct a discussion. Again, this involves the teacher in doing three things:

1. Encouraging change in the groups themselves, so that the pupils have the chance to work with other pupils;
2. Encouraging talk about how the discussion progresses, what helps and what hinders it, and how else it might be organized;
3. Illustrating other models through the teacher's own style of teaching.

Secondly, it pin-points the central issue of children being encouraged to see what they do as itself *a stage in learning,* and not a final stage. They were asked at the beginning of the session, as we have noted earlier, to decide, among other things, on those parts of the text which they found difficult, but there is a sense in which, at least, for some of the group, the major difficulty is not finally resolved. This is not to say that there is no progress made. To the contrary, there is a great deal of progress. But the discussion does finally highlight how much encouragement children need in order to be absolutely open and insistent about what they do not understand.

In the next chapter we take the discussion of reading a stage further by looking at a small group of children who are working at a 'cloze' comprehension test taken from a passage they have previously studied.

6
Reading:
Group Discussion of a Cloze Test

Introduction

In a cloze reading test, the readers are given a passage from which every ninth word or so has been deleted. The test is to close the gaps appropriately with a single word in each case.

The Schools' Council project on *The Effective Use of Reading* makes a specially strong case for groups working together on such tests. What follows is an example of a group of 12-year-old boys working together on such a test, as part of their work in science. The test follows considerable discussion about the passage as a whole from which the test is taken. Also, this discussion is their *second* endeavour at the same task. They have already worked together on the same test and have had that work marked and returned by the teacher. They have done well at this first attempt; they have scored 16 out of 20; had they done less well, there would be fairly little value in doing the test again so soon. There has been, though, no further work on the passage or on the test between the first and second attempts.

As we have said, the boys are 12 years old. Their reading ages according to a Widespan reading test, are, with one exception, strictly average. David, Rajesh and Derek have reading ages of 12, while Joe has a reading age of 14.

The passage they have been working on is concerned with two major theories of the origin of the universe - the Big Bang and the Steady State theories. According to the Flesch method of testing its linguistic complexity, it requires a reading age of 21 or thereabouts.

The Test

Here is the extract (from the passage) used for the cloze test:

> **Physicists attacked the Steady State theory, ridiculing the - (1) - of the creation of matter out of nothing by means of - (2) - unknown process. It seemed to do violence to - (3) - laws of physical nature, and it was**

forgotten - (4) - this is just what the Copernican theory had - (5) - in its day. Some mathematicians did not favour - (6) - hypothesis either, but it could only be proved true or - (7) - by observation, and it was here that the radio-astronomer really - (8) - into his own. The detection of radio waves - (9) - outer space had been made first in 1931, - (10) - their significance was unappreciated. Only after the Second - (11) - War was their importance recognized by the majority of - (12) - . By the 1950s enough progress had been - (13) - in the design of radio telescopes to enable - (14) - sky to be mapped, and Martin Ryle at - (15) - was able to announce that his observations showed - (16) - at very great distances in space there seemed - (17) - be more galaxies than could legitimately be explained - (18) - the Steady State Theory were correct, but which - (19) - be anticipated on the Big Bang Theory. Yet - (20) - radio-telescopes record no visual image, these results were open to question since it was possible that not all the objects detected were galaxies. In the event it became clear that this was so. The questions of which theory was correct remained open.

The group's first attempt at the test produced these results:

1. hypothesis	11. world
2. an	12. scientists
3. the	13. made
4. that	14. the
5. stated	15. NASA
6. this	16. that
7. false	17. to
8. came	18. that
9. from	19. would
10. but	20. the

The teacher marked all of these answers as acceptable except for numbers 5, 18 and 20. (He queried number 15, adding that this was something that could be discussed later.)

The Discussion

David:	*'And it was forgotten that this is just what the Copernican theory had - ? - in its day'.*
Rajesh:	*You put down* stated *and he marked it wrong.*
Derek:	*Could it be* said?
Rajesh:	*'Said in its day.'* (5)
David:	*Hold it. 'This is just what the Copernican theory had. . . .'*
Derek:	Said?
Rajesh:	Said? - *'Had meant in its day'?*
Derek:	*No. Don't sound right.*

David:	*Now go back to number 4 and read up the sequel to*	(10)
	that. Number 3, sorry. 'It seemed to do violence to the	
	laws of physical nature, and it was forgotten that this	
	is just was the Copernican theory had. . . .'	
Joe:	*'Done in its day.' Cause up there - 'It seemed to do*	
	violence.' And the theory has done violence.	(15)
Derek:	*Yeah. Could be.*	
Rajesh:	*Yes.*	
Derek:	*Sounds right.*	
David:	*What other word could there be for done?*	
Rajesh:	*Stated is wrong . . . Said?*	(20)
David:	*Proved?*	
Rajesh:	*Well it would either be proved or said or done.*	
Joe:	*Let's go through them all, then.*	
Rajesh:	*'This is just what the Copernican theory had proved*	
	proved its day.' Dosen't seem to sound right.	(25)
Joe:	*'This is just what the Copernican theory had said in its*	
	day.'	
Derek:	*Can only be one word can't it?*	
Rajesh:	*No not really. Cause other people have probably put in*	
	loads of things, haven't they. Like number 15 - univer-	(30)
	sity, college - they're all right.	
Joe:	*Well I say done.*	
Derek:	*Okay, we said it fits, didn't we.*	
Rajesh:	*Number 18 we got wrong. We put that.*	
Derek:	*Go back to number 16.*	(35)
Rajesh:	*'. . . his observations showed that at very great distances*	
	in space there seemed to be more galaxies than could	
	consistently be explained by the Steady State Theory	
	were correct. . . .'	
David:	*Don't sound right.*	(40)
Rajesh:	*No. So let's leave that for a moment.*	
Joe:	*No.*	
David:	*No, let's get it done with now. '. . . his observations*	
	showed . . . there seemed to be more galaxies than could	
	legitimately be explained - '	(45)
Joe:	*'. . . that the Steady State Theory were correct, but*	
	which would be anticipated on the Big Bang Theory.'	
Derek:	*Yes.*	
Joe:	*Let's think . . . we said number 19 was would and we got*	
	a tick for it.	(50)
David:	*'. . . than could legitimately be explained by the Steady*	
	State Theory.'	

Rajesh:	*No.*	
David:	*If?*	
Derek:	*'If the steady state theory were correct.' That sounds*	(55)
	right.	
David:	*Yeah. More galaxies could legitimately be explained if*	
	the Steady State Theory were correct.	
John:	*No.*	
Rajesh:	*'. . . but which would be anticipated on the Big Bang*	(60)
	Theory.'	
David:	*Yes: I agree there. I think it should be* if. *Put it down as*	
	number 19 - no, number 18.	
John:	*Number 19 is* would.	
Rajesh:	*We put* could *and then we crossed it out and put* would	(65)
	down.	
Joe:	*Yeah. But it could be* could *as well. . . .*	
David:	*What did we put for number 20?*	
Joe:	*The - and we got it wrong.*	
Derek:	With *radio-telescopes?*	(70)
Joe:	*With?*	
David:	*'With radio-telescopes record . . .' No. Doesn't sound*	
	right.	
Rajesh:	*What about -* 'Do *radio-telescopes record no visual*	
	image.'	(75)
Joe:	*It would still sound all right if there wasn't meant to be*	
	a word there. 'Yet radio-telescopes record no visual im-	
	age. These results were open to question since it was	
	possible that not all the objects detected were galaxies.'	
	What about if?	(80)
David:	*It sounds right. But then in a way it doesn't.*	
Rajesh:	*Yeah. Depends on the way you read it.*	
David:	*But if you read on, it doesn't seem right.*	
Joe:	*'Yet the radio-telescopes record no visual image.' I still*	
	think we should put that down though. 'Cause it was the	(85)
	first thing that came into our heads. I can see that.	
Rajesh:	*Yes. 'All radio-telescopes . . .?'*	
David:	*Yes. 'All radio-telescopes record no visual image. These*	
	results were open to question . . .'	
Rajesh:	*Yes, I reckon it's* all. *Cause it means all over the world*	(90)
	- the whole universe.	
Joe:	*I think we ought to try for some more. There might be a*	
	better one.	
David:	*So.* All. *Now what - what word can explain the word*	
	all?	(95)

Joe:	Everything. *Every one?*
David:	*Yeah.* Every *radio-telescope. . . .*
Derek:	*No. Doesn't sound right.*
Joe:	'Any *radio-telescopes . . .*' *No.*
Derek:	'Every *radio-telescope . . .*' *No. Doesn't sound right.* (100)
Joe:	'Anyone. . . .'
Derek:	*No.*
David:	'Every . . .' *doesn't sound right.*
Derek:	*If it was just* any *radio-telescopes that would have sounded right.* (105)
Joe:	*Yeah. That would have sounded right.*
Derek:	*Yeah, but when you read on - 'Yet* any *radio-telescopes record no visual image, these results were open to question.' Doesn't sound right.*
Rajesh:	*There should be a question mark or something,* (110) *shouldn't there?*
Joe:	*Yeah. Something like a question mark or exclamation mark after it. Like number 10. That had to have a comma before it.*

(Long pause)   (115)

David:	*'Yet* some *radio-telescopes. . . .'*
Rajesh:	*No. I don't think it's* some. *I think it's* all.
David:	All - *yes. But we've got to think of some more, cause we couldn't agree on that word.*
Derek:	*Yeah.* (120)
David:	*We've got to think of a better word.*
Rajesh:	*If you say* 'some' *right? It seems to say that it doesn't concern* every.
Joe:	*Yes. It seems to say that there are some that can record visual images. That's what it suggests. That's no good.* (125)
Rajesh:	*Yeah.*
David:	*Well. We'll think of that later. Let's go back to number 5. If there's a vote to see what you think of number 5. . . .*
Rajesh:	*Yes. Number 5.*
David:	*What do you think number 5 could be? What do you* (130) *think first of all, Derek?*
Derek:	*'. . . and it was forgotten that this is just what the Copernican theory had - ? - in its day.'*
David:	*What do you think?*
Joe:	*I think it's* done. (135)
Rajesh:	*Yeah.* Done.
David:	Done.

Joe:	*Cause people attacked it then, just like people are attacking it now.*
All:	*'. . . it was forgotten that this is just what the Coper-* (140) *nican theory had done in its day.'*
Rajesh:	*If you read from number 3, it's all got to make sense. It does.*
David:	*Yeah. Put down* done.
Derek:	*Right.* (145)
David:	*Number 20. That's the hard one.*
Joe:	*Listen to this. 'Yet* all *radio-telescopes record no visual image. These results were open to question since it was possible. . . .'*
Derek:	*Yeah. That sounds right.* (150)
Joe:	*Yes. I agree.*
David:	*We'll go back over it. But we'll just put it down for now.*
Derek:	*What other one haven't we got now?*
Joe:	*Just number 20 and number 5.* (155)
Rajesh:	*But what did we put for number 18?*
David:	*If* wasn't it?
Rajesh:	*We put down* that. *That was wrong. Yes. Should be* if.
Derek:	*I agree. Right?*
Rajesh:	*Yes. Gotta be. Number 5 is* done. *'Cause 'it seemed to* (160) *do violence - ' at number 3. So it's done violence.* *'Cause read from number 3: 'It seemed to do violence to the laws of physical nature, and it was forgotten that this is just what the Copernican theory had* done *in its day.'* (165)
Joe:	*Yes. It's* done. *I definitely agree.*
Derek:	*I'd prefer some other word.*
David:	*But it fits in there, like.*
Rajesh:	*Now what else have we got wrong? Oh, we're back to number 20. What else did we think for number 20?* (170)
Joe:	*'All radio-telescopes. . . .'*
Derek:	*Doesn't really sound right.*
Rajesh:	*I'm not really quite sure. Well, what do you think, Joe? Do you think it's* all? *Does anyone think it's* all?
Joe:	*Well, it could be. That is very probable, but I think it's* (175) *something else.*
Derek:	*A bit better. More accurate.*
Rajesh:	*Yeah . . . I can't think of a word though.*

(Long pause)

David:	Can *radio-telescopes. . . ?*	(180)
Rajesh:	*Gotta be a question mark any way.* Can? If?	
David:	*I think* all *sounds right.*	
Rajesh:	*Yeah.* All.	
Joe:	*It sounds all right. But we still need a better one.*	
David:	*A bit harder. More accurate. And more precise.*	(185)
Rajesh:	*Yes.*	
Joe:	*We'd probably get a better one if we tried.*	
Rajesh:	*Let me think. Hang on. The word* world-wide - *is that just one word?* 'Yet worldwide *radio-telescopes. . .*'	
Derek:	*Yeah. It's only one word.*	(190)
Joe:	*Yeah, it's one word. Not* world wide. *But* worldwide.	
Rajesh:	'Yet world-wide *radio-telescopes. . . .*'	
Joe:	*It could be.*	
David:	*It's a possibility*	
Joe:	*We'll keep that in mind.*	(195)
David:	*Yeah, put that down, Derek. Note it down.*	
Derek:	*Well let's have a preview. I forgot to ask Joe what you think of number 20?*	
Joe:	*I reckon it could be* all. *But it could be like something else we've said, like* world-wide.	(200)
David:	*And what do you think, Rajesh?*	
Rajesh:	*Well. . . .*	
Joe:	*I don't think it's anything like* nation-wide. *You see, we're not talking about places like Russia. They don't get on well with America, so it probably would not be* nation-wide.	(205)
Rajesh:	*Could be* nation-wide. *You never know.*	
Derek:	*I reckon there could be loads of things.*	
Joe:	*Yes. So I reckon we should try every single one, until we find one that is really good. Right?*	(210)
Rajesh:	*What do you think about it, Derek?*	
Derek:	*I reckon it could be* world-wide.	
Joe:	*Yes. Round the whole world.*	
David:	*What we're trying to say is - 'cause we're not the only ones in this world. You know, everyone. Not just one nation.*	(215)
Joe:	*So, If there's going to be a catastrophe, one nation isn't going to keep it for itself. So* world-wide.	
David:	*Yeah, that's right.*	
Rajesh:	*What about* all? *That seems right as well. That's still* world-wide.	(220)
Joe:	*We could get an idea if we . . .*	

Rajesh:	*Hang on. Take this theory, right? If it was American, right? - No, that couldn't be it. One telescope couldn't be better than another.* (225)
Joe:	*Could be.*
Derek:	*No. Listen.*
Rajesh:	*The Russian could be better than the American. They got satellites earlier.*
Joe:	*You've got a point there.* (230)

The next part of the taped discussion is very difficult to decipher. They appear to talk about different ways in which America and Russia might be superior, technologically, to each other. Derek breaks this by suggesting they now reread *the whole passage* with the new words they have now talked about. In so doing, they stop at number 2 because Joe reads the answer as *some* instead of *an*. The latter has already been marked as correct.

David:	*Number 2. It can't be* some.
Rajesh:	*Why not?*
David:	*If it was* some, *it would have to be* some processes. (235)
Joe:	*It could work either way.*
Rajesh:	*Hang on.*
Joe:	Some process. *It could be either.*
David:	*I reckon* some. . .
Derek:	*I go for* some *too.* (240)
Joe:	*I think it's* some. *But what if it could be something else? Could be* an. *But there could be three alternatives. Could be three or four.*
David:	*Same with number 20.*
Rajesh:	*Be better if we used a dictionary.* (245)
	(Consulting the dictionary) *We'll look up* some.
	Equals - several, few, little, certain.
Joe:	*What was the first one?*
Rajesh:	Several.
Joe:	*If it was* several *or* few it would be processes. That's the (250) rules of English.
David:	*Could be* sophisticated. *Sophisticated unknown processes.*
Joe:	*Give us the dictionary. I'll look up* an.
Rajesh:	Some *means* few. *And if it was* few *it would be* (255) unknown processes. *So why wouldn't* some *be* some unknown processes? *As you said, it's the way English is spoken.*

Joe: *Listen to this:* An - *meaning* one. *The indefinite article*
            used before words beginning with a vowel. Another.'   (260)
Rajesh: *You see: Meaning* one. *Would one fit into number 2?*
Joe: *Quickly, think of another word that could go in that.*
            We should think of one other word that could go in
            there and then look it up in the dictionary.
Rajesh: *Well, can you think of anything?*   (265)
Derek: *No. I can't.*
Joe: Some *seems right. You can't argue about it.*
Rajesh: *I think it'll have to be* some. *Both the answers are right,*
            so we can't really argue. (Everyone laughs!)
Derek: *So we're back to number 20. Let's read it through* (270)
            again. From the beginning. (Derek does this, reading all
            for number 20, and also reading the comma after the
            word image *as if it is a full stop.)*
Derek: *'All' - it still doesn't sound right!*

At this point they run out of time. It is the end of the lesson.

Commentary on the Discussion
There is again, a specific range of factors at work here.

Their Thinking
The discussion is mostly concerned with producing three correct answers.
They succeed with two, number 5 (*done*) and 18 (*if*) and fail with number
20. It will be useful to try to compare the thinking behind these answers.

Taking Their Time
The central factor running right through their discussion is their willingness
to keep on trying, to consider every possibility, to listen to each other, and
to put each other's ideas to the test. In the case of number 5, they go
through a number of possibilities: *said, meant, proved,* and then settle for
done. It is Joe who first suggests *done,* at line 14, quite rightly taking his cue
from the earlier part of the sentence where the theory is said to *do* violence,
and hence the second theory mentioned (the Copernican) will be likely to
have *done* the same thing. It is David who in part helps him towards this
solution by reading out the entire sentence, as opposed to concentrating
purely on the phrase in which the missing word occurs. Joe then makes the
logical connection between the two parts of the sentence, for in effect it is
'doing violence' that is the central idea of that particular sequence.

Derek and Rajesh appear to accept Joe's answer, saying that it 'sounds
right'. David asks if there could be any other word similar to it, and this
leads to only one more suggestion, from David himself, namely, *proved.*

They then reread the sentence putting in first, *proved,* and then *said.* Interestingly, no one points out that in their first draft they had written down *stated* and that it had been marked as incorrect, and that there is little meaningful difference between stated or said or (less certainly) proved. However, Joe repeats that it is most likely to be *done,* and they appear to accept this, and then move on to other things.

Apparently, though, not all of them are convinced at this stage, for later, David asks them to go back to number 5 - at line 127. Joe repeats his answer, and his explanation, and they all together read the second half of the sentence (from the comma) and agree that it is correct, Rajesh commenting, 'If you read from number 3, it's all got to make sense. It does.'

In the case of number 18, they first move back to an earlier part of the sentence (but not to the beginning of the sentence) and work their way from there onwards. They go through this latter part of the sentence several times, considering the possibility of using the word *by.* It is David who then suggests *if,* and the others seem to accept this straight away, with Rajesh reading aloud that particular part of the sentence with *if* incorporated into it. They remind each other about this answer very briefly, a little later on - at about line 158, but they do not argue it further.

The rest of the discussion is devoted to the elusive number 20, apart from an intriguing aside which is devoted to a reconsideration of one they have already had marked as right, but which they suddenly realize could reasonably be something else. In their work on number 20 they do as much as, and indeed more than, they do on the ones they manage to get right. For example, they go through an impressive range of possibilities, including - *with, do, the, all, every, if, any, some, can, world-wide,* and *nation-wide.*

The Whole and the Parts

It is impressive that all the members of the group refuse, at some point, to accept answers that they cannot fully come to terms with. They all, in this way, relate the various 'parts' to the whole of the passage, testing an answer by its plausibility in its actual context. Thus David rejects *if* (at line 83) because, 'if you read on, it doesn't seem right'. Similarly, Joe is able to make a positive suggestion in reply to every solution put forward by the others, while also keeping the field open: 'I think we ought to try for some more. There might be a better one' (line 93). And a little later, 'It sounds all right. But we still need a better one' (line 184) and, 'We'd probably get a better one if we tried' (line 187). And later, when Derek says, 'I reckon there could be loads of things', Joe replies, 'Yes, so I reckon we should try every single one, until we find one that is really good. Right?' (line 210). And they continually reject answers that, while they appear to make broad sense, do not seem to fit accurately into the passage. Thus Derek rejects *every* because it doesn't sound right, and on the same criterion rejects *any* (line 104) and is not too happy about the absolute correctness of *done* for number 5 (line 167) but cannot think of a substitute. Similarly, Rajesh makes the important point that there is not necessarily any *one* answer (line 29) and later establishes why the word *some* would be an inaccurate answer, as contrasted with *all* (line 117). It is also he who introduces the dictionary at a later stage, and who makes the point that both their answers to number 2 must be right, 'so we can't really argue' (line 269). In a similar vein, David at one point asserts the need for an answer that is, 'A bit harder. More accurate. And more precise' (line 185).

The Word and the Sentence

In one sense, though, they do *not* consistently relate the part to the whole. They do not always place their suggestions in the context of the *entire sentence*. For instance, although they read the entire passage more than once, they do not, while working on number 18, reread the entire sentence in which it occurs. It is very possible that they do this to themselves, silently, but they do not check the process by reading it aloud together. In this sense, their success with number 18 has an element of sheer luck to it. But the luck deserts them with number 20. This occurs in a much shorter sentence. Joe reads out the whole sentence, on its own, only once. This is in the early part of the discussion, at line 76, and he appears to misread its punctuation, reading the comma as if it is a full stop. He appears to repeat this mistake later, at line 147, where he only reads part of the sentence, but again reads the comma as a full stop. They engage in a very careful and lengthy discussion of the possibilities, but they do not again read the sentence as a whole, nor does anyone question Joe's reading. It is at least possible that if all of them had insisted on placing their ideas in the context of the whole sentence, and read it out accordingly, then they would at some point have moved to the correct solution.

Working Together

They work together remarkably well. Each one at various times, takes the lead, and they are admirably relaxed in allowing each other to do so. Their disputes are all good-natured, as when David rejects Rajesh's suggestion that they leave number 18 to return to it later: 'No, let's get it done with now' (line 43). Likewise, they all agree to Derek's suggestion that they reread the entire passage at the end (line 270). It is noteworthy, too, that they are also able to vary the rules, as it were, of the game, for they accept Rajesh's proposal to introduce the dictionary, and they then proceed to make good use of it as a group. And perhaps the most sophisticated convention is their acceptance of the possibility of there being more than one acceptable answer, and further, that *no* answer is better than an answer to which they cannot honestly assent.

Language Used

They are very language-conscious, very aware of words and interested in getting them 'right'. Thus they argue the possibility of *world-wide* being two words or one word, though they do not explore the possibility of its being hyphenated (line 191). They show a talent for working out synonyms, especially in relation to number 20, and also show a definite concern for linguistic correctness - as when they discuss whether it is acceptable to talk of *some process* as opposed to some *processes*. It is important to note that they engage in this particular discussion, and go to the dictionary to help them to resolve the issue, despite the fact that they already have a correct answer for this particular question, and the answer has already been marked by the teacher. In this sense, their pursuit of the issue is a marvellous example of children pursuing knowledge for its own sake. They do not need to know in order to get a right answer for the teacher's sake, since they have already found an alternative right answer. They carry on to resolve the problem because they want to do so. The problem itself, a purely linguistic one, fascinates them.

In fact, the dictionary does not resolve the matter for them. It provides them with a number of synonyms, but does not appear to establish the accuracy of Joe's suggestion that *some* can be followed either by the singular or by the plural. Nor does Joe himself then go on to give other examples which might clinch the matter. Instead, David and Derek accept his idea, and Rajesh later does also, though without any further proof or demonstration having been added. In the meantime, Joe has pointed out that the *rules* of the language require the plural to follow *few* or *several,* and Rajesh clearly thinks the same rule should apply to *some* (line 256). They are then side-tracked into an exploration of the meaning of *an,* but they do not return to the more interesting, and more relevant problem, of devising or suggesting a possible other rule that would allow a word such as *some* to be followed by singular or plural words.

It is impressive too, that they do not seem to be taken aback by the complexity of some of the language in the passage, and they use some similarly complex language in the course of the discussion: *hypothesis, legitimately, theory, sophisticated, catastrophe,* and *preview* (in mistake for *review,* at line 197) are among the various concepts they deploy usefully at one point or another.

They are less secure in regard to *punctuation.* Rajesh thinks that the statement that, 'these results were open to question' should be followed by a question mark (line 110). Joe follows this by suggesting it could be followed by a question mark or an exclamation mark. In the same sentence, Joe has already made the mistake of reading the earlier comma as if it is a full stop.

Reading Difficulty

As with the group of 11-year-olds whom we looked at in the previous chapter, these children are able to make considerable sense of a passage which is, by one criterion, many years too advanced for them. They talk about it, resolve many of their difficulties in understanding it, and make fair progress towards wrestling even with those difficulties which still, in the end, elude them.

Knowledge Used

It is interesting that although they bring to bear a fair amount of general knowledge on the various issues raised by the test, including such things as the nature of theories and hypotheses, they do not at any point seek to spell out or to ask each other - *what is a radio-telescope?* In part they seem to *assume* that they all know, and in part to assume that it is *irrelevant.* Throughout all the thinking about number 20, they do not stop to ask each other - 'what does a radio-telescope do?' or, 'what is a radio-telescope?' Thus, it is not made clear from the discussion itself whether or not they all understand or agree that radio-telescopes actually record *no* visual image, or how they function at all. A lot of the time it seems to be implicit in their observations that they have, as it were, got it right, as when Rajesh talks about the situation pertaining 'all over the world' (at line 90) and when Joe agrees that *some* is not acceptable as an answer because, 'It seems to say that it doesn't concern every' (at line 123). But it is difficult to be sure since they never make it explicit and do not ask each other about it. For instance, at one point Joe also suggests that the answer could be *if,* and they all reject this without rooting their decision in any statement about the telescopes themselves. They simply say, '. . . it doesn't seem right' (line 83). Also, and perhaps because they are not bothering to spell out the nature of radio-telescopes, they do not seek to relate the significance of the absence of visual images to the questionable deductions that are to be drawn from the findings of such telescopes.

Very possibly this is more the fault or inherent danger of the exercise than the fault of the group themselves. Cloze tests inevitably focus our attention on individual words within a passage, and tend to get us thinking about 'right' words rather than the wider field of knowledge to which the passage relates. Hence, we may tend to forget that individual words are to a large extent determined by context and subject-matter, and a necessary part of finding the 'right' word is checking the subject-matter itself. Certainly, with this particular group, the focus is essentially a linguistic-semantic one. They are mostly talking about words that make sense, rather than about the topic itself. And there is a fair case for arguing that this is a basic risk in cloze tests, and one that teachers have to be aware of, and seek to guard against.

In fact, though, they do *start* to connect the passage, and specifically the part they are finding difficult, with their knowledge of its context - at line 213. Here they are discussing for a second time the possibility of using *world-wide,* and they agree that this would be a better word than *nation-wide,* on the basis, if we are reading them correctly, that radio-telescopes are to be found all over the world. As a result of this, they argue, whatever a radio-telescope picks up in one part of the world will, in effect, become available elsewhere. This appears to lead Rajesh (at line 223) briefly to consider the possibility of using *American* as the appropriate word, but he rejects this on the grounds that one country's telescopes will not be better than another's. When Joe disputes this, he corrects himself by noting that Russian telesopes might well be better than the American ones since they 'got satellites earlier' (at line 229) But they are still not asking - 'what do we know about radio telescopes? What are they?'

The Teacher's Role

Two specific points arise from this particular discussion. The first is the need for practice in looking carefully at what is read and in talking critically and precisely about the text itself. This may be a matter of constantly relating a word to the sentence in which it occurs, and then to the paragraph, and then to the whole passage. In essence, this is again a question of relating *the parts to the whole,* and *the whole to the parts,* and of doing so without suddenly losing sight of either. Thus, just as the group in the previous chapter overlooked the key word 'only' at a vital stage in the proceedings, so the group on this occasion misread a similarly vital piece of punctuation. The irony is that this particular group also show a very commendable determination to reread the *whole passage* before finally deciding on their answers. But they do not persevere with the *offending sentence as a whole,* i.e. the sentence containing number 20. They do not try to paraphrase the whole sentence in their own words. They do not go beyond a paraphrase of the clause itself, down to the comma. As a result, their attention does not focus on the word *since,* and this is also the word that correctly closes the gap at number 20. *Since* is the answer they look for and do not find. And their failure to do so is largely the result of their reluctance to focus on the sentence itself and then on the passage as an entirety. This is something they can be taught to do.

Secondly, the discussion shows the importance of relating a text to what one knows about its subject-matter, and hence of establishing what each other does actually know. This may mean, as a deliberate technique, taking central concepts and ideas from a passage and asking each other about them. Also, as the obverse side of the same coin, there is the importance of establishing what one does *not* know, the questions that remain to be pursued. Hence, on some occasions, children may very usefully be invited not to answer parts of (or even an entire) cloze test, but rather to list the questions they would like to discuss before they feel they know enough to set about the test itself in a meaningful fashion. Such a technique can help to shift the emphasis from the purely linguistic to a wider canvas of knowledge and understanding.

We can now seek to bring together some of the points we have made about these two discussions, and place them in a more geneal context of the teaching of reading across the curriculum.

Summary: Reading Across The Curriculum

1. There is a real need for reading to be taught right across the curriculum, not simply to aid the development of reading skills in general, but to help children to master each subject within the curriculum. The children in both the discussions we have used here, are very much engaged in thinking about the text in front of them. Their success varies, but they all make very clear attempts to understand something new and complex.

2. Group discussion is a useful approach to the reading of a text, including group discussion of a cloze test as well as of a passage as a whole. At the same time, in the various ways which we have indicated, children can be taught to engage in group discussion more effectively.

3. Complexity of the language itself is only one factor in the overall complexity of reading a text, and while reading ages and reading-difficulty scores are useful guides to a teacher, they are not to be observed too literally.

4. One of the major difficulties for the reader of any text is of relating what he or she knows already, to what the text appears to be about. In fact, the greatest difficulty in this connection seems to be to recognize what we, the readers, do *not* know, and it is our failure to recognize this that finally defeats us. In other words, it is essential to encourage readers (and talkers and writers also) conscientiously to ask questions, and just as conscientiously to talk about the answers.

5. The two discussions we have used here also illustrate the way in which effective reading demands precision from the reader. Sometimes this precision is lost because the reader moves too rapidly from the part to the whole. In fact there has to be a constant back-pedalling: from word to sentence, from sentence to word; from sentence to passage, from passage to sentence. This is a complex process, and requires a lot of practice.

We now move on to an activity that is very much related to reading and talking, as well as to writing - children making their own notes.

7
Making Notes

Introduction

This short chapter is a postscript to the preceding chapters on talking and reading, as well as an introduction to the following (and concluding) chapters on writing.

The making of notes is an intrinsic part of learning, and helps us to extend and to build on what we gain from reading, and from talking and listening. It helps us to do this independently of whether or not we are planning to use what we read and listen to, in some form of extended writing. Such notes are probably the most personal kind of writing in which we ever engage, in that they are meant solely for our own eyes and our own use. They are also indispensable. Most of us, whether sophisticated students or inexperienced beginners, retain remarkably little of what we meet in a lesson, a lecture or a book (or, for that matter, in a film or television programme, or conversation). Our notes later become the central thread that leads us back to certain parts of the original material. Without the notes we are lost.

The school curriculum tends to place a lot of emphasis on taking notes, i.e. writing them down at dictation or copying them - but tends to neglect the making of notes by pupils themselves for themselves. In fact, there is an important place for both note-taking and note-making.

We have in mind here the making of notes as part of the work on some kind of literary text, rather than the making of notes 'out of one's head', without any kind of text, as the prelude to, say, writing an essay.

What is the teacher's role in helping children to make useful notes?

The Knowledge Used

To be able to make notes on anything is a matter of knowing something about it to begin with. In effect, it involves having in mind some kind of question to which the text can provide an answer.

The Children's Questions

So a useful trial run in note-making may be a session where children devise their own short list of questions on a given topic, and then listen to material, that, at least in part, provides some of the anwers. Here is an example of the questions drawn up by a group of 11-year-olds just before being given a talk by the science teacher on the 1980 *Voyager II* space probe to the planet Saturn:

Questions about life on Saturn

1. Is there life on Saturn?
2. Are theories about life on Saturn shattered by the space probe?
3. Would there be enough money for research to enable man to live on Saturn? Would the government agree to spend the money on such a project?

Questions about the organic make-up of the planet

1. What is the actual land like?
2. What does its atmosphere consist of?
3. What gases are there in Saturn's atmosphere?
4. If Saturn was formed at the same time as our own planet, why is its make-up different from ours?

Questions about the space probe itself

1 What is a space probe?
2. How did it get to Saturn? Where will it go next?
3. Who is in charge of the space probe?
4. Have men been in the space probe?

Questions about the universe generally

1. Will Saturn come to an end?
2. Does the universe go on forever? If so, can we ourselves imagine an unending universe?
3. How big are the planets? Which ones are the biggest?
4. What does Saturn look like? Does it look different from other planets?
5. How and why did Saturn, or any of the other planets, become itself?

After discussion with the whole class, the above questions were then reduced to three key questions which seemed to represent the interests of most of the children, and they then listened to the talk.

By using the children's own questions, the teacher at least partly ensures that children are beginning to make links between their own experience and the subject-matter of the text itself.

The Language of Note-making

Since we make notes for ourselves, we can, of course, employ our own abbreviations, our own shorthand. This may involve, for instance, sessions where the teacher asks children to go through notes they have already made and see if they can usefully reduce the length of words and phrases and sentences, perhaps mixing standard forms of abbreviation with those of their own devising. It is also useful to establish that the rules of punctuation are not applicable to notes, and that not only is the sentence, as such, unnecessary to note-making, but also that punctuation can be pressed into whatever service is of use to the note-maker.

Ways of Thinking

Note-making is a form of summarizing: it involves editing, revising and abbreviating the text itself. It is in this way the most thoughtful of activities, demanding a neat balance between *economy* (keeping the note as brief as possible) and *precision* (getting the point, clearly - seeing 'the wood' and not being diverted by 'the trees'), and between the *whole* (the central idea of the text) and the *parts* (the specific point or points that the note-maker is looking for), and between *creativity* (finding for yourself the best way of expressing the point in your own language) and *correctness* (making sure that the note does actually express the point you are looking for). The teacher can help on all three levels.

Economy and Precision

Anyone when first asked to make notes, is likely to try to write down everything, regardless of how much they already know and of how much they may need to refer to later. So one aspect of the teacher's job is to encourage children to select and discard, perhaps having sessions where a short passage is read to them and they are asked to select one word or short phrase from the passage that seems to summarize, contain the germ of, the point they are looking for. Group and class discussion will have an important part to play in this activity. Further sessions can concentrate on the children finding their own words and phrases rather than finding them in the passage itself.

The Parts and the Whole

In effect, note-making is harder as the number of component parts increases. In other words, making notes from a range of evidence is in essence a more daunting task than making notes from one source. Similarly, it is also more daunting, all other things being equal, to make notes on a discussion than on a lecture, because the various contributors increase the field of the activity, adding to the number of parts to which the note-maker must attend. In this way, making notes on a group discussion of which you are yourself a member is an even more sophisticated exercise.

Notes are made to be used, and it is worth adding that *using* them makes a different set of demands on the note-maker. To some extent, he or she has to reconstruct from the notes a new version of the original text and then fashion that to the task at hand which may, for example, be writing a discursive essay or a newspaper report. So there is an important place for more elementary exercises where the form in which the notes are used is fairly close to the form of the notes themselves, as when pupils have been asked to note three points with a view to reporting them in note form on some kind of questionnaire. Similarly, the shorter the time-lapse between making and using notes, then, all things again being equal, the less daunting a task it is.

Creativity and Correctness

A task becomes more creative, the farther away it gets from simply finding what is already there. In broad terms, evaluating the underlying theme of a story is more creative than spotting the specifics of character and plot. Hence there may be a place, even within one lesson, for a range of tasks for the note-maker to perform, so that there is some chance to build confidence by doing something that is less demanding. At the same time, it is only by engaging with something that is difficult (for the learner) that there can be scope for being creative.

Ways of Working

One of the best ways to make notes is by working on them as a group and talking about them. Note-making is an essential part of group discussion; the two activities complement each other.

It is useful for teachers to set up sessions where pupils make notes on texts they *listen* to, and separate sessions where the notes are on texts they *read*. The two activities make different demands - possibly a text that is well read *to* the class is slightly easier to comprehend, and to attend to critically, than a text that is read by the individuals themselves. But both are valuable tasks.

The temptation when making notes is to make them too soon - to start making notes before the whole text has been in any way assimilated, and hence, possibly to miss the relevant moments when they occur. The teacher can train children not to do this by having sessions where they have to listen to or read the whole passage before doing anything at all. Making notes while actually reading or listening, is a more sophisticated task.

Similarly, it is helpful to have sessions where the material, after being read, is taken away, so they cannot even refer back to it.

Making Notes in a French Lesson

In the following example, a class of *12-year-olds* make notes and then use them in the *French* lesson. They have been studying French for just over a year. In the course of this lesson they read a story, make notes on it, dramatize part of the story and then, working in pairs, write about any part of the story they happen to like.

This is the *text of the story,* which they were asked to read to themselves:

'Vous avez fait un bon voyage? Et comment va votre mère? Est-ce que son rhumatisme lui donne encore beaucoup de douleurs? Entrez dans la maison, mes enfants.'

Tante Jeanne demande toujours des questions. On n'a pas besoin de les répondre. Chaque année en juillet Marc et sa petite soeur Julie partent pour un petit village en Bretagne où ils passent leurs vacances chez leur Oncle Claude et la Tante Jeanne qui est la soeur de leur mère. Claude et Jeanne habitent une petite ferme très isolée près de la mer. Parfois Claude invite Marc d'aller pêcher avec lui.

Les enfants s'installent dans leur petite chambre et ils descendent dans la cuisine où Tante Jeanne prépare un bon dîner. Comme ils sont fatigués après leur voyage les enfants se couchent de bonne heure. La mer est un peu houleuse cette nuit; il y a un assez fort vent et les nuages cachent la lune. Soudain Marc se réveille; il entend un certain bruit qui vient d'en bas. Marc va à la fenêtre ouverte; il ne veut pas réveiller sa soeur qui dort paisiblement. Il entend deux hommes qui parlent mais il ne peut pas les comprendre. Ce n'est pas son oncle. Il décide d'aller voir ce qui se passe. En marchant sur la pointe de ses pieds il descend, ouvre la porte et il sort. Heureusement, Milou le chien qui garde la porte le connaît; il agite sa queue et il accompagne Marc. 'Sh. Milou, ici, reste ici,' Marc chuchote. Milou est bien obéissant; il reste à côté de Marc. Les deux prennent le sentier qui mène jusqu'à la mer. Au bout du sentier il y a une petite cabane de pêcheurs. Son oncle a le droit d'y entrer et d'y garder quelques appareils pour son travail. La mer fait encore beaucoup de bruit; Marc pense aux pauvres pêcheurs en pleine mer par une nuit comme ça. En passant près de la cabane il voit une lampe clignotante au vent; il s'approche de la cabane. Milou commence à gronder.

'Sh, Milou, reste tranquille, ce n'est rien.'

Il tient le chien par son collier. La porte de la cabane est ouverte; il y peut distinguer deux hommes en manteaux de caoutchouc qui examinent une boîte sur la table. Il y a beaucoup de petits paquets avec quelque chose de gris ou de brun dedans. Les poils de Milou sont hérissés et son nez commence à renifler. Marc voit comment les hommes remettent les paquets dans la boîte. Après ils enlèvent une planche et cachent la boîte au-dessous de la planche. Ils quittent la cabane et ils passent tout près du garcon et du chien cachés d'un côté. Marc est très curieux. Il rentre silencieusement et le lendemain il raconte l'aventure à son oncle. Celui-ci appelle un gendarme immédiatement et tous les trois suivis par Milou se rendent à la cabane. Voilà une grande trouvaille de drogues: Le chef de police remercie Marc en public; ce soir-là on l'interviewe à la télévision et, ce qui est le plus important, on lui donne une récompense de mille francs. Il en est bien content. Il attend avec impatience la fin des vacances pour raconter cette aventure à ses camarades.

N.B. clignotant - flickering.

After reading the story to themselves, they were asked to read it a second time with a partner and briefly to chat about it. The copies of the text were then handed in, and the children were then asked to do the following:

1. Working with a partner, to make rough notes of any words or phrases they particularly remembered, in any order they liked;
2. As a class, to compare their notes, with the teacher putting the various words and phrases of one pair on the blackboard and asking the class to compare these with their own;
3. To suggest a suitable title for the story; the most popular suggestion was 'L'Aventure d'une Nuit';
4. To dramatize Marc's television interview and the reward ceremony;(there was a solemn procession with Marc accompanied by his uncle, his aunt, his sister, his parents and neighbours; he was interviewed, given his reward and publicly congratulated. Throughout this, the children kept very largely to the vocabulary of the story itself);
5. Finally, they were asked to use their rough notes, again working in pairs, to write about any part of the story they particularly liked or remembered.

David and Paul made the following rough notes from which they worked out their first draft of the story:

ici, reste ici	*tante Jeane est la soeur*
oncle Claude	*de leur mère*
tante Jeanne	*ils dort paissablement*
c'est rien	*ils se couche de non heures*
cabane	*un rćompense*
la mer (près de)	*mille francs*
très isolée	*un interview à la Télévision*
un bruit	*en vaccane*

Soudain Marc se réveille	allz vous (!!)
Heuresment	Un boite
tante Jeanne prépare un	un lampe cloignate
bon diner	chaque année
	les pêchurs

And this was their first draft of the story:

UNE NUIT D'AVENTURE

Marc et sa souer, ils vont passer les vacances en Bretagne. Ils vont chez oncle Claude et Tante Jeanne qui habitent une ferme très isolée pres de la mer. Marc, il va pecher avec son oncle. Oncle Claude a un chien qui s'appelle Milou. Les enfants sont très fatigué quand ils arrivent, ils vont se coucher de bonne heure.

Dans le nuit Marc se reveille parceque il entend un bruit. Il se leve et descend. Il ouvre la porte et le chien Milou vient avec lui. Marc et Milou vont à la cabane òu ils ont voient une lumiére. La porte de la caban est ouverte. Ils voient deux hommes avec des paquets gris et brun. Marc et Milou va vite à la maison pour telephoner le police. Le police arrive et ils arrestent les drogues. Marc est un garcon tres courageux, et les police donne lui une recompense. Cette nuit, Marc est sur la television. Le recompense est mille francs et Marc est trés content.

By contrast, Rachel and Lucy made the following notes:

LA NUIT D'AVENTURE
(Jottings)

En juillet Marc et sa soer passer l'vacance à le petit ferme de l'Oncle C. & Tante J. Il est pres d'mer & il est tres isolee. Les enfants se couchent à bon heure le mer fait de bruit.

Soudain M. se reveille parce qu'il entende deux homme qui parle. Il ne comprende pas. Il ne se revielle pas sa souer qui dorm pacibliment. Au pointes de pieds il descend l'escalier et avec le chien d'Oncle C 'Milcu' il quitte la maison.

'Rest ici Milou' il dit. Milou est trés obeissant.

Il voit une lumiere clignotant dans une petit cabane. Il se cache et voit le deux hommes par le fenetre overte. Il entende l'homme qui parle. 'Ou est les drogues.'

'Voilà' dit l'autre homme. Marc voit un boite de paquets avec quelquechose brun et gris dedans.

L'homme chache le boîte sous un planche de cabance. Marc rentrer à la maison vite. Il racontre l'envent à Oncle C qui telephoner les gendarmes. Ils attrapent les contrabandiers et Marc est interviewer au télévision. Il receive un recompense pour mille francs au public.

And this was their first draft of the story:

En juillet, Marc et sa souer vont passer les grands vacances à le petit ferme d'Oncle Claude et Tante Jeanne. Le ferme est près de la mer et il est très isolée.

Les enfants se couchent de bonne heure. Le mer faire de bruit et les nauges cachent la lune.

Soudain, Marc se reveille parce qu'il entend deux hommes qui parlent. Il ne comprende pas. Il ne se reveille pas sa soeur qui dort paisiblement. Au pointes de pieds il descende l'escalier et avec le chien d'Oncle Claude Milou il quitte la maison.

'Reste ici. Milou', il dit. Milou est très obeissant.

*Il voit une lampe clignotant dans une petite cabane. Il se cache et voit les deux hommes par le fânetre overte. Il entende l'homme qui parler.
'Où est les drouges?'*

'Violà' dit l'autre. Marc voit une bôite de paquets avec quelquechose brun ou gris dedans. Les hommes cachent le bôite sous un planche de cabane. Marc rentrer vite à la maison.

Il raconte l'aventure à Oncle Claude qui téléphone les gendarmes. Ils attrapent les contrabaniers.

Marc est interviewer au télévision. Il receive un recompense au public de mille francs.

David and Paul follow the original story fairly closely, and display a command of French that is remarkable for their age and for the fairly short period of time they have been studying the language. They leave out of their first draft such details as 'tante Jeanne prépare un bon dîner' and 'tante Jeanne est la soeur de leur mère', even though they have included them in their notes.

The interview and the public reward ceremony receive short shrift in their version and also in Rachel's and Lucy's. This is probably because the improvisation has already done full justice to those parts of the story.

Rachel and Lucy are perhaps more adventurous. Their rough notes already show a strong desire to tell a story - instead of listing words and phrases they write a continuous sequence. Even so, there is remarkable progress between the rough notes and the first draft, and they obviously have a great feel for the language. 'Ils attrapent les contrabaniers' is pure invention in this context, and is remembered with affection from elsewhere.

The whole session seems to have fulfilled its aim (at least in some measure) of providing children with an opportunity to read, talk and write French, to use the language with greater confidence. And the note-making has played an important part in the whole activity.

Summary

Note-making is an important part of learning, and needs to be used right across the curriculum. The teacher can help children to make useful notes by encouraging children to ask questions of a text before they actually read or listen to it; by helping them to think about the note-making in different ways, moving from the less difficult to the more difficult; and by organizing the work itself in conjunction with varying activities. Most especially, note-making is a part of discussing and reading texts in groups, and in effect represents a link between talking and reading on the one hand and writing on the other.

It is to children's writing that we now turn, looking especially at two kinds of writing - *stories,* and the *discursive essay.*

8

Writing: The Short Story

Introduction

Of all the forms of literature that are employed in the adult world, it is the short story that is the most widely used in the school curriculum. From about the age of six or seven onwards (in other words, as soon as children are more or less able to read) they are asked to write stories, and this continues throughout the primary and then the secondary school, with perhaps a slight tailing off in the last year or two when other kinds of writing possibly supercede it. If you could count up the number of stories school children write as part of their school work, each individual child would probably write an average of at least one a week, which over ten years adds up to about 400 stories. Quite possibly, with a very literary child, fluent and assured on paper, the total is even higher. Some of these stories are original, written in response to the teacher's invitation that children write a story for story-writing's sake. Some of them are summaries or recapitulations of stories thay have been told or they have read. Some of them are anecdotal, personal explorations of things that have happened to the writer. Some of them are 'true' stories from history. And so on. But they are all stories.

In the course of writing this vast number of stories, how does the child's language develop? Or does it develop at all? and What is the teacher's role in this?

One Child's Story-writing in 5 Years of Secondary Schooling

To help us explore these questions, we look at examples of stories written by one boy, *John,* over a period of 5 years in the secondary school. We reproduce here *one* story for each year, taking him from age 11-plus to age 16-plus. The stories represent work in English (language and literature) and history.

Year 1 (Age 11 - 12) A Story Written in English

THE OLD HOUSE

The rain came down and the lightening flashed I didn't have my coat so I ran for shelter. The house was eerie and the dark trees groped down like long boney fingers in the night. I could see the shadowy dark house close by, then suddenly the lightening flashed, the house was lit brightly and for a second I thought I saw something. It was so (5) *creepy I was going to go home. But down came the rain very heavy, so heavy that I had to go in. I was scared stiff, even petrified at the horrific sight in the hall: A dead body, Blood stained with staring eye's, staring into nothing. Then suddenly at the top of the broken down staircase appeared a shadowy figure, clad in a dark cape. An eerie* (10) *laugh cut through the cold air and a deep voice boomed around the old house. 'Welcome to the house of Dracula.' I thought quickly, what can I do. I mustn't panic, what can I do. I know. Panic! I ran blindly through the house. I ran through dark cobweby rooms faster and faster. Where can I go. I pulled open a door and found myself* (15) *face to face with Dracula. I stared into his face and saw the long white fangs stained with blood from the body in the hall, the short hair coming to a point in the middle of his forehead. I ran again back the way I came but I stopped dead as right in front of my eyes he materialised from nowhere. Without thinking I grabbed two broken bits of wood* (20) *and held them up in the sign of the cross. Dracula stepped back covering his pale face. The power of the cross was holding him back. Then I noticed that one of the sticks was pointed. I took down the cross and He started forward so I drove the stake through his heart. He yelled with pain as the stake came out of his back. He fell back and lay* (25) *lifeless on the floor.*

I wasn't going to stay in the house a momment longer. I got to the front door and ran like the wind through the storm. I didn't stop untill I got home and I was never going back to the house again.

Year 2 (Age 12 - 13) A Story Written in History

THE SACRIFICE

One day I was taking my ass along the track that led to the capital (30) *aztec city Tenlochatan when five Aztec warriors in their frightening battle dress jumped out on me from a bush, it was an ambush. They picked me up and carried me off while one of them stabbed my ass to death. I was thrown into a cell made of stone with no windows except for one in the door. Inside this cell were lots of desperate people not* (35) *wanting to be sacrificed. At sunset the Aztec priests came and took a screaming man away. I got to the window in the door and looked out.*

They dragged the man up the steps of the pyramid and laid him on a slab. As the sun went behind the pyramid it cast a long dark shadow over most of Tenlochatan. There was a blood curdling scream and a (40) *priest held a bloody heart up to the sky. A minute later two Aztecs came past the door bearing a lifeless bloody body on an old piece of wood. I felt sick.*

That night I hardly slept, with the thought that tommorrow I would just be a sacrifice to the sun. At sunrise they came for me but as the (45) *priest opened the door I kicked it back in his face his sword stuck in the door and I ran at him. He fell on the floor and I yanked his sword from the door and ran it through his heart. I ran faster and faster over the cursed city of the Aztecs. Aztec warriors were on my tail but I was desperate and I out ran them all. I travelled accross land for six weeks,* (50) *on foot, and I reached the sea.*

There were strange ships on the shore and I went to them. The men on the ship had a strange way of talking they took me to their leader whose name was Cortes. He and his men managed to communicate and I led them to the city of the Aztecs to get gold. (55)

Year 3 (Year 13 - 14) A Story Written in English

THE SMASH AND GRAB MYSTERY
'Bye.' said Peter as he left his friends on the corner of the High-street. 'Bye!' said Jim, Gary and Paul. Peter walked off down the street, with his dog by his side.

Peter walked on until he came to the traffic lights at the junction. Joe, his spanial, sat down at the kerb (he was well trained) and they waited (60) *for the lights to change.*

Suddenly Peter heard a crash, it came from the side ally next to the jewellers shop. What was that! He ran down the road past the shoe shop and Luigi's ice-cream parlour and looked round the corner into the alley. Two men were standing at the window, with shattered glass (65) *on the pavement around their feet. One of them was short and fat, the other was tall and strong, they were grabbing the watches, rings, necklaces and brooches from the shop's window display. A 'smash and grab' robbery!*

Peter stood there rooted to the ground! What should he do? The men (70) *threw the jewellery into a sack and started to run up the alley, then they spotted him. 'Grab 'in' yelled the fat man. Peter overcame his fright and started running, but it was too late. In no time at all the tall man was upon him. 'Gotcha!' grunted the man as he grabbed Peter by the collar.* (75)

Peter was dragged back to the fat man, there was nothing he could do

the man was big and strong. 'We'll have to take him with us, Jack!'
said the fat man, who was obviously the boss.
They bundled Peter into their getaway car, a black Ford Cortina (80)
driven by a skinny man who had big round glasses and it sped off up
the road. It skidded into a side road and pulled up sharpley as the
skinny man slammed on the brakes. Peter was pulled out and into a
green Renault. The driver (the skinny man) turned the key and put his
foot down. The Renault zoomed away and turned into the North
Dock Road. . . . (85)

The narrator is taken to a warehouse near the docks, where he is tied up, gagged and left for hours on end all on his own. Suddenly he hears a dog barking. It is his own dog, come to the rescue. The narrator struggles free, cannot get out of the locked room, and so writes a note, stuffs it into an old cigarette packet, and throws it to the dog. Eventually, the dog takes the message back home, and the police arrive on the scene just in time to save the narrator from death by drowning. The whole story is approximately 2200 words in length. It ends in this way:

Some time later they were all at Scotland Yard. 'Well done!' said the
Superintendant to Peter and the boys. It's not us you have to thank,
it's Joe. After all, he did deliver my S.O.S. and catch what was his
name - Fat George Burke!' said Peter.
Joe barked his agreement. (90)

Year 4 (Age 14 - 15) A Story Written in English

STAN

Stan sat huddled in a doorway wrapped in a few old newspapers to
keep warm. His collection of rubbish that he thought might come in
useful sat in two carrier bags in the opposite corner of the doorway
together with his few possessions which he still held on to.
He watched a young couple pass by on the other side of the road (95)
carefully not looking in his direction and he wished he could be an ac-
cepted person in society again.
It wasn't often that Stan was sober for very long, and when he was he
always felt this way - sad, lonely, and reminiscent. He wished to
himself that he had never started drinking. It had started with a few (100)
pints in the pub and an occasional drunken night, then when he turned
to whisky, scotch and gin in order to forget his troubles he had been
unable to stop. Now he was unemployed and unable to afford
anything more than meths. What he would give, he thought, to be liv-
ing an ordinary life, like so many other people were, and not to be (105)
treated as an outcast to be looked down upon.

*'No-one cares what happens to me,' he said to himself. 'I can't even
walk into a cafe to buy a cup of tea, they just tell me to move on and
usher me out of the door.' He put his hands in the pocket of his dirty
overcoat, the cold October wind was numbing his fingertips. A greasy* (110)
chip paper tumbled past on the pavement.

*'Even the police have stopped bothering with me now,' he told
himself. 'They've given up trying to get me into the hostels. I just get
my soup and the odd proper meal there sometimes, but I couldn't live
there - not without my drink.' He wished he had a bottle now, could* (115)
forget about everything and stop feeling sorry for himself.

*He thought how everybody walked by him, as though he didn't exist
or they didn't want him to exist, except for the gangs of small boys
who sometimes teased and abused him - and felt even more lonely
than before. He wished again for a bottle of something.* (120)

*He was shivering with the cold of the wind and the grey concrete step
beneath him and he decided not to stay there any longer. He bundled
his papers into one of the carrier bags and shuffled off along the road.
Maybe he could find the other meths drinkers on the old bomb-site.
Perhaps they would have a fire going and a bottle of meths with which* (125)
he could drown his sorrows.

*Year 5 (Age 15 - 16) A Summary of a Story Studied in
English Literature*

LOT - BY WARD MOORE

*America is being attacked. A nucler bomb has been dropped on Pitts-
burgh and another on the Los Angeles area.*

*The Jimmon family live in Malibu near L.A. The family consists of
Mr David Jimmon, Mrs Molly Jimmon and their three children Jir* (130)
(16) and Wendell - the two boys - and Erika (14).

*Mr Jimmon has planned for this moment beforehand and they have
packed all the essentials into their station wagon so that they can drive
out into the wilds and survive there. They will hunt and fish and live
on rabbit, squirrel, abalone and fish.* (135)

*On the morning of the nuclear strike the water and electricity have
gone and the Jimmons decide to depart.*

*Leaving their dog behind to fend for itself they drive to the freeway to
join the stream of fleeing refugees. From there they head south and
then northwards past Santa Barbara.* (140)

*However, from the very beginning, Mr Jimmon's family begin to an-
noy him. They refuse to accept what is happening and will not let go
of their old way of life. Mrs Jimmon keeps thinking of petty things
such as whether they remembered to turn the taps off should they have
phoned Dan and Pearl, Wendell keeps on about his dog, and con-* (145)

tinually pesters his father to stop at a gas station with a toilet. Jir is generally sarcastic and unhelpful. Only Erika acts sensibly.
By skill, daring and judgment, Mr Jimmon manages to get his family in their station wagon a good way in front of the rest of the refugees pressing behind, but finally he has to stop at a filling station. (150)
After filling the tank, the petrol costing 5 dollars per gallon at these black market prices, he decides to abandon his family. He sends Molly to go and phone Dan and Pearl, giving her 200 dollars to put in her handbag. Then he sends Jir and Wendell after her, and he and Erika drive away. (155)

In discussing the developments in John's story writing, we will use the same basic model as before, looking at:

1. The attributes of his *thinking;*
2. The kinds of *knowledge* he employs;
3. His use of *language.*

We cannot talk here about his ways of working, for we only have the end-product and no evidence of the work that preceded it. Obviously we could make a number of deductions about how he worked, but we are more concerned with the *general* implications for teachers in their use of the short story as a means of learning.

Ways of Thinking
To what extent does the child writing a story operate within recognizable constraints? And to what extent can we see the child thinking his or her way through these constraints?

The Formal Structure of Narrative
Another way of putting the same questions is to ask - Is there an underlying structure which, regardless of how much we may or may not be aware of it, characterizes all narrative? One of the most interesting answers to this comes from the American linguists William Labov and Joshua Waletsky. They made an extensive study of oral narratives, and concluded that virtually everyone, when invited to tell a story, whether long or brief, creates different clothing for what is essentially the same underlying form. According to their findings, this underlying formal structure has five different components. These are:

1. *Orientation* - that section of the narrative which introduces the listener to the context of the story, including perhaps the main characters, the central action and the mood;
2. *Complication* - the setting up of a series of events that in various ways complicate the action of the story;

3. *Evaluation* - the introduction of some sort of authorial comment into the story. This may simply be to stress the element of, say, tension and excitement, or in the case of an autobiographical anecdote, it may be to stress the teller's own merits. These evaluative elements generally break up the strictly temporal sequence of the narrative;

4. *Resolution* - the bringing of the action to a close;

5. *Coda* - a functional device for bringing the narrator and the listener back to the present time and thus for rounding off the experience of listening and talking.

Labov and Waletzky argue that these formal elements are part of all, or virtually all, oral narratives. The exceptions are remarkably few and are not specific to particular age groups. Indeed their analysis is based on stories told by people of all ages, from 10 to 70. Of the five elements which they establish, the *coda* is a little less common than the others. It is by way of being an optional extra. In many cases it is no more than the briefest of comments, such as - 'And that's that!'

This formal analysis of the components of a story is, as we have said, based on the composition of oral narratives, not written ones. The written story will tend to be different in a great number of ways. It will tend, for instance, to be longer, to involve greater complexity of action and of characters, and the evaluative element will tend to be more ambitious. Even so, within the relatively short form of story writing employed in most work at school, one would expect the same basic structure to be apparent - *orientation, complication, evaluation, resolution* and *coda.*

Formal Structure of John's Stories

Following the work of Labov and Waletsky, one would expect to see the same formal structure to all of the stories across the period of the five years during which they were written, with a development, if any, in the kinds of thinking the writer brings to his stories. How far is this true?'

An *orientation* occurs at the beginning of each story. The first one starts with - 'The rain came down and the lightening flashed. . . .' In this way the writer instantly establishes the context for the events that are to follow. In later stories the central characters and actual locations are introduced just as immediately.

In each story the events are at some point *complicated*. The fight with Dracula; the arrest and impending sacrifice; the seizure by the thieves; and the irritations presented to Jimmon Senior by the rest of the family: all these create problems to be resolved within the narratives. The fourth story is formally very different. There is only one character, and the action takes place mostly in his mind. Stan watches a couple go by; he communes with himself; feels cold; feels thirsty; gets up and goes. The complication here is internal. It is Stan's conflict with himself; his self-pity, his regrets, his despair that lead him to get up, move on and find another bottle of meths to drown his sorrows.

The *evaluative* elements in a story can exist on two levels: there is first, the level of the character's own attitude to and evaluation of the events; there is secondly, the level of the writer's attitude. In all these stories John fundamentally identifies with the character, and indeed it is only in the last two stories that he writes in the third person as opposed to the first, though even in these last two stories he is again identifying with his protagonists. The evaluative element is firmly established in each tale. Thus in the first story he observes - 'It was so creepy . . . I was scared stiff' (line 7); in the second he writes of, 'the frightening dress . . . the blood-curdling scream . . . the desperate people'; in the third he describes how 'Peter stood there, rooted to the ground! What should he do?'; and in the fourth he writes that Stan is 'sad, lonely and reminiscent' (line 99); while in the fifth tale the central character is annoyed by the 'petty things' that absorb the rest of the family. (John misses, though, a second layer of evaluation - the author's own attitude - a point which we return to later.)

In each story there is a clear *resolution*. Dracula is destroyed; the Aztec escapes; Peter's dog brings the police; Stan moves on; Jimmon abandons his family.

There is a *coda* at the end of the first story - '. . . and I was never going back in the house again.' A more elaborate coda concludes the second, with the hero, having escaped, meeting Cortes and leading him back to the city. And the last five or so lines of the third story also constitute a full coda to the preceding resolution, with the dog being congratulated and barking his approval. The last two sentences of the fourth story beginning, 'Maybe . . .' and then, 'Perhaps . . .' fulfil the same basic function, showing in effect that life goes on; the end is only the end of the story, but Stan carries on.

There is no coda to the last story, though it could be said of John's summary, as of the story that his is summarizing, that the question of what happens to the family that are left behind is the very central, but implicit, coda to the tale. In effect, if the reader is not left wondering this, then the story has been ineffective.

In effect, then, John has a clear grasp, right from the point of entry into the secondary school, of the formal elements around which to write a story; he has the clear basic structure around which to think. What are the attributes of the thinking itself?

Economy and Precision

All the stories are economically written. There is very little repetition or padding. To the contrary, he is able to develop and extend his ideas rather than pad them out arbitrarily. Thus he can write, 'I was scared stiff, even petrified . . .' (line 7) and, 'It skidded into a side road and pulled up sharply as the skinny man slammed on the brakes. . . . (line 81). He is also consistently *precise*. There is never any doubt or confusion as to who is doing what, or to whom, or where or when. He is even fully aware of the need for such precision, hence the explicit bracketed aside in the third story - 'The driver (the skinny man) turned the key . . .' (line 83). Similarly, in the final story, he keeps control of the collection of characters and locates them all in their various actions without causing any difficulty for his readers. Indeed the fifth story is a major performance, capturing the essential details of a long, short story (a story of about 10 000 words) in less than a twentieth of that length.

Correctness and Creativity

Story writing is a marvellous opportunity for the writer to create his or her own world, but within the constraints of an underlying formal structure. In effect, the creativity cannot function without such structure. So there is a sense in which, even in a story, standards of *correctness* apply. John achieves this correctness in all the stories. As we have noted already, he is able, right from the start, to create, complicate, evaluate and resolve his narrative ideas. In none of the stories does the narrative get lost or abandoned.

He is also very *creative* in his thinking. In the first story we have the fine collection of images to establish the mood, such as - 'The house was eerie and the dark trees groped down like boney fingers in the night . . .' (line 2) and the equally atmospheric - 'As the sun went behind the pyramid it cast a long dark shadow over most of Tenlochatan . . .' (line 39 in the second story). Later he writes of Stan being 'sad, lonely and reminiscent . . .' (line 99) and pin-points his feelings nicely, with the image of the greasy chip paper tumbling past on the cold pavement, thus bringing together, briefly and pithily, the varied components of Stan's condition - hungry, grubby, cold, dilapidated.

The Parts and the Whole

To what extent is he able, at different times, to create stories where different *parts* come together to form a *whole* - for example, to relate setting to character and to mood? Or to show the relationship between two quite different episodes? Or to create counter-themes and sub-texts? It could be argued that, in some such respect, the second year story is more complex than the first, in that the story has a decisive break in the middle before launching into a new sequence of events and the arrival of a dramatic and new set of characters. This development is sustained in the following story where there is a sequence of self-contained scenes, each with its own development, and each locking into the next. And even more ambitiously, in the fourth story, there is the interlinking of the outward events and the inward experience of Stan as he interprets those events. Finally, in the fifth story, the writer achieves the major feat of reducing a long 'short' story to a brief summary, while managing to retain (a) the central sequence of events and (b) what he sees to be the central theme of the story. This is a difficult balancing act, in that he must repeatedly move backwards and forwards through the various parts and the over-arching 'whole'.

It is in this respect, then, that the thinking expressed in his stories show the clearest development.

Knowledge Used

The writing of a story involves drawing most especially, but not exclusively, on one's knowledge of people - how they behave and why. This knowledge is itself drawn from two main sources. One is the writer's own experience of people in the everyday world. The other is the writer's experience of people in the various art-forms which in one way or another tell stories about people, such as novels, comics, television drama and films. In between these two great sources of knowledge lies a third, which is in part both of them together and in part neither of them, and this is the experience one has of people by way of rumour and gossip and myth and report, and which much of the time resists classification as either fact or fiction. All three sources become part of one's knowlege of people, and thus become part of our thinking and part of our story writing.

The first three of John's stories are quite firmly wedded to a genre that could be called heroic melodrama and show fairly little observation of particular, individualistic behaviour. The stories inhabit a land of stereotypes where everyone behaves predictably. Dracula is destroyed by the hero; the Aztec traveller walks into an historical adventure of historic proportions; the schoolboy is caught by thieves and saved by his excellent dog. Even so, they all have moments of unpredictability. Thus, in the first story there is the anti-heroism of the hero's sudden panic; in the third story there is the similar moment when the hero is too scared to move and hence loses the brief opportunity to escape.

The fourth story is a different matter. The detail with which Stan's consciousness is filled in, is richer and more complex than anything in the previous stories. His response to seeing 'a young couple pass by . . .' (line 95); the fact that even the police have lost interest in him; Stan's resentment of the way people try not to notice him, except for 'the gangs of small boys who sometimes teased and abused him . . .' (line 118) - all suggest an imaginative awareness of people's behaviour and a real ability to project himself into the derelict's feelings. In terms of the knowledge he utilizes, this story goes beyond a confident knowledge of specific narrative genres into a wider knowlege of human motivation. He is not simply portraying a stereotype, he is bringing to the story a definite curiosity, and ranges with some freedom across his own experience in answering the question - What is it like to be someone like Stan? This is not to say that in this story he necessarily draws on direct experience of having actually known a derelict, though this is not entirely impossible. To the contrary, he is probably drawing on insights rooted in films and documentaries, stories and poems and in comments he has heard made by friends and relations. But it seems at least possible that in putting his portrait together he is deliberately extending the knowledge he considers relevant. It is notable, for instance, that he does not attempt to involve other characters in the story, and hence does not engage Stan in some 'obvious' adventure where the focus is on what happens rather than why.

In this sense the fourth story also marks a change in the writer's values. He no longer takes it for granted that overt action is the essentially interesting thing about people and life. The covert experience of thinking and feeling is beginning to assume priority. The first and the third stories show momentary interest in the anti-hero; the fourth story takes this much further; in the fifth story he is summarizing someone else's story in which the central character is virtually the complete anti-hero, who leads his family away from a nuclear disaster, only to abandon all but one of them because they get on his nerves. The essential feature of the original story is the motivation for Jimmon's action, which is depicted in fairly complex terms. In his summary, John has, of course, to select a central thread from all this complexity, commenting, 'They refuse to accept what is happening and will not let go of their old way of life' (line 142). This is perfectly fair comment on the story and on a part of Jimmon's motivation, but it is interesting that he entirely leaves out the fact that it is the wife's expressed concern for her friends, Dan and Pearl, that encourages an old suspicion that she has been unfaithful with Dan and that one of their children is actually Dan's and not Jimmon's. Hence, the final act of leaving his wife while she goes off to phone Dan and Pearl is heavily ironic.

It is possible that one reason why John picks out the hero's irritation with his family's behaviour, but misses the sexual antagonism, is that he does not yet know anything of sexual antagonism. He will quite probably know what adultery is, and know what suspicion is. But he perhaps does not yet know how powerful a suspicion of adultery can be within a husband and wife relationship. And it is worth adding that he would need to know this fairly unambiguously to be able to do full justice to the motif of adultery in the story, for Jimmon is shown as a character under great stress, whose imagination and suspicion are running away with him. He is himself a sick man. Hence, the reader cannot be absolutely sure whether his suspicions are correct or not. Indeed he seems so obsessed with them, and yet has done nothing about them until now, that on balance he is probably wrong and also quite mad. But the fact that the writer never makes this explicit, renders it all the more easy to miss the point. If this is a fair interpretation, and it is not necessarily a correct one, then the summary shows a lack of understanding of a major aspect of human behaviour. (We are not saying he *should* understand it, nor that the story is therefore unsuitable for him to read or study.)

At the same time, John does capture in his short summary the equally central fact that it is the collection of small details, in the context of the nuclear disaster on the horizon, that drives the hero to his act of desertion (in effect, an act of murder). The motivating force is not one big, simple factor, but many small, complicated and interrelated ones. And John travels a fair way towards representing these in his summary.

So it could be said that the stories written in the fourth and fifth years reveal a developing awareness of the complexity of human behaviour. He is moving to some extent away from a melodramatic view of stories and of the characters who inhabit them.

Language Used
And what kind of development can be seen in the language itself?

Length of Units
It does not seem that the various linguistic units get longer as he goes from one year to the next. Neither words nor sentences seem to lengthen noticeably, nor do the stories as a whole. Also he employs some quite complicated sentence structures even in his first story, as with the sentence beginning, 'I was scared stiff . . .' (line 7) and, similarly, he uses some quite sophisticated words and phrases such as, materialized, horrific, eerie and 'clad in a dark cape', 'an eerie laugh cut through the cold air. . . .'

Errors
The writing contains a number of errors. The most common error is in failing to find the *punctuation* that renders the sense of what is written so absolutely clear that the reader does not have to do any repunctuation for himself or herself. But it is worth stressing that at no time does he write anything that the reader cannot make sense of.

In the first story the sentence beginning, 'I was scared stiff . . .' (line 7) contains the sophisticated (and correct) use of a colon, but he then follows this with a capital letter, and 'Blood', a little later, is also given a capital. The question - 'What can I do?' is twice written without a question mark, as is the question - 'Where can I go?' The word 'He' is written with a capital 'H' though it is not the beginning of the sentence (line 24).

In the second story there are cases where he presents two sentences as if they are one, running them together without any division. This happens in line 32, after 'bush', where there needs to be either a colon or a full-stop. And in line 46, there needs to be either a comma or a full-stop between the words 'face' and 'his'.

Similarly, in the third story there should probably be a full-stop, not a comma, in line 67, between the words 'strong' and 'they', and similarly in line 71 between the words 'alley' and 'then'. The same applies in line 76, between the words 'man' and 'there'. And in the same line (76) there needs to be a full-stop after 'do' or alternatively, some link word such as 'because'. There is also the need for a comma after the word 'glasses' in line 80, to mark off the end of the description of the car and its driver and to distinguish it from the succeeding action.

In the fourth story, the errors are less unambiguous. There needs to be a comma between 'useful' and 'sat' in line 93, and after 'road' at the end of line 95. And there should probably be a full-stop, not a comma, in line 108, between the words 'tea' and 'they', and again in line 110 between the words 'overcoat' and 'the'. On the other hand, he can present the rather complex sentence beginning, 'He thought . . .' (line 117) and cope successfully with its punctuation, including the use of the two commas and the dash. In the final story, the punctuation seems entirely correct, apart from the rather complex sequence beginning (line 143), 'Mrs Jimmon keeps thinking of . . .' This could be kept as one sentence, as John presents it here, but the markers between the different items should probably be semi-colons rather than commas.

As regards actual words, the only error that occurs anywhere is in the first story (line 14), with the use of 'cobweby' - a perfectly logical mistake, but a mistake nevertheless. There is no such word.

As regards spelling, in year 1 John slips up on *lightening, momment* and *untill.* In year 2, on *tommorrow* and *accross.* In year 3, on *sharpely* and *superintendant.* And there are then no spelling mistakes in year 4 or in year 5.

Hence, there is some evidence that his linguistic correctness does actually improve over the years, and that he can check himself more easily from running sentences into each other, from mis-spelling words, and from using non-existent words. But it is significant that even here, the progress he makes across the years is negligible compared to the progress he has made *when he starts* working at the secondary school. The first story is remarkably well spelt; it is well punctuated, and even contains a colon correctly used to introduce a sequence of noun phrases in apposition to the preceding 'horrific sight'. Elsewhere in this story, the writer correctly uses speech marks to distinguish direct speech, and an exlamation mark to mark off the cry of 'Panic!'

Summary: The Learner's Development

1. From the beginning of his secondary schooling, at the age of 11, John's language was in every sense well developed. He had a clear command of the narrative form, and could write thoughtfully and interestingly, developing and sustaining his ideas.

2. Later he shows a developing awareness of the complexity of human behaviour, in life and in art. He seems to be moving away from stereotypes towards a more thoughtful viewpoint.

3. Related to this movement, is an increasing ability to juggle with a number of diverse ideas without losing the line or unity of the story. In particular, there is a more deliberate interweaving of covert and overt action, of what is felt and thought, with what is actually done.

4. His written language becomes increasingly 'correct'.

5. The developments that occur are in no sense continuous and consistent. To the contrary, there seem to be times when he is repeating himself, when much the same attributes are in evidence from one year to the next, and without any very apparent change. The development between the third and fourth years is greater than developments elsewhere.

We will leave for the moment a discussion of any implications for the teacher. Instead we will look now at the development of *discursive writing* by the same writer over the same period of time. We will then try to draw together the implications for the teacher in relation to both kinds of writing - narrative and discursive.

9
Writing: The Discursive Essay

Introduction

Discursive writing explores some kind of problem without having any axe to grind, votes to win or prejudice to display. Its central concern is to think carefully, internalizing different points of view, admitting fresh evidence. It is to be found in various guises, including academic writing, journalism and official reports. It is also to be found, as a kind of bracketed aside, within other forms, as when the narrative line of a memoir or novel is temporarily departed from, to allow the writer to explore certain points more fully for their own sake. Discursive writing always tends to be complicated, to demand an amount of patience and care on the part not only of the writer but also of the reader, for it is virtually *looking for* an alternative line of thinking, reluctant to settle at the point it has reached, reluctant to conclude.

At the same time, since all thinking about any problems endlessly opens up ways of solving that problem, *discursive* writing naturally moves towards *persuasive* writing, towards persuading the reader to do something, to accept the conclusion reached. (Needless to say, a lot of persuasive writing spends very little time being discursive.) In addition, since any kind of discursive writing involves the exploring of evidence, and hence, to some extent, the presenting of such evidence, it also naturally moves towards *informative* writing. Again, though, a great deal of informative literature allows little, if any, time for being discursive.

To be able to write discursively about something, involves the writer in assembling what he knows about it and in thinking carefully about the problem in relation to what he knows. It obviously has, therefore, a major role in the school curriculum.

One Child's Discursive Writing in 5 Years of Secondary Schooling

Here are examples of the discursive writing of the same pupil, John, whose short stories we looked at in the last chapter. We reproduce here two examples of each year's work, from the age of 11 to the age of 16. The examples are drawn from work in science, history, geography, sociology, chemistry and English language and literature.

The actual quantity of his discursive writing seems to have increased as he got older. There was very little in his first year, at age 11 or, to be more precise, there was very little in such of his work as we were able to see. Even so, there was some work which showed, even then, a sort of embryonic discursiveness, and we include this in our examples.

It must be stressed that we are here reproducing work which seems to us to be *in part* discursive, and we are then examing its discursiveness. This is not the same as claiming that the work was intended by the teacher, or the pupil, to be discursive at all. Very possibly, much of the work was primarily intended to be informative, with the pupil re-expressing, in his own language, material that had already been worked on in other ways in the class. All we have done here is to take two examples, from each year of the child's work, which most embodied discursiveness, and in that sense were outstanding. John had kept many, but not all, of his exercise books, so we had a fair sample to select from, but inevitably we were not able to select from all his work.

Year 1: Two Examples of John's Work in Science

1(a). THE WORLD IN THE FUTURE

In about the year 4000 I think there will be about twice the amount of people in the world. People will live in high rise flats and the offices will also be skyscrapers. Everyone will travel by jet, monorail or hovercar. Meals will be in the shape of tablets (like the astronauts eat). Because there will be so many people some will live under the sea. (5) *They will live in water tight houses and travel in mini submarines, and on aqua scooters.*

1(b). AN EXPERIMENT TO EVAPORATE TAP-WATER

Apparatus (the writer has sketched a Bunsen burner standing under a tripod, and has marked on the sketch - watch-glass, beaker, tap-water, water and wire gauze.)

Method *We set up the apparatus as shown in the diagram. The bunsen burner was lit and the water in the beaker heated this in turn heated the water in the watch glass. The experiment was continued until all* (10) *the water in the watch glass was evaporated.*

We evaporated the water in this way to prevent the watch glass from cracking.

Results *At the top of the experiment a white solid was left in the watch glass.* (15)

Conclusion *Tap water contains disolved solids.*

Year 2: Two Examples of John's Work in History

2(a). CAUSES OF THE ARMADA

There were 3 mains reasons for the Armada:
1. *Religion,*
2. *Mary, queen of Scots, and*
3. *English sea captains, like Drake who raided Spanish property.*   (20)

King Philip II of Spain was a Catholic and he wanted to make everyone Catholic. He had been married to Mary Tudor, a Catholic like himself, and she tried to make him her heir. When Mary died Elizabeth I became Queen, Elizabeth was a Protestant and she made England Protestant again. So Philip of Spain, wanting to make (25) *England Catholic, asked Elizabeth to marry him. Elizabeth refused him, she had no intention of marrying anyone, let alone Philip, for he was Catholic.*

The Dutch who were protestant were under Spanish rule and they were rebelling against Philip. This rebellion was aided by the English who (30) *gave Dutch sailors safety in English ports on the East coast and also had soldiers fighting alongside the Dutch.*

Mary Queen of Scots was, like Philip, a Catholic. When she fled to England from Scotland she was imprisoned. Some people said that Mary Queen of Scots had a right to the throne and King Philip sup- (35) *ported her. Philip was accused, along with the English Catholic leaders of plotting with Mary against Elizabeth I. Mary Queen of Scots was executed and this annoyed Philip.*

Another thing that annoyed the Spanish was raiders or pirates, especially Francis Drake. The English ships raided ports of the (40) *Spanish colonies in America, they attacked Spanish treasure ships and stole the gold and treasure that was going from Spanish America to Spain. There was also the slave trade. The Spanish raided Africa and captured negros as slaves, then they took them back to Spanish America to work as slaves. The English also captured negros and took* (45) *them to the Spanish in America. The Spanish did not like the English interfering with their slave trade.*

Francis Drake did all of these things and more. Once he was forced into the Pacific after raiding some Spanish ports in America. He sailed up the coast of South America raiding Spanish ports as he went. These (50) *Spanish though they were safe from attack. From there Drake sailed right round the world in his ship, which had been called the Pelican but the name was changed by him to the Golden Hind. Once Drake sailed into Cadiz harbour and did a lot of damage to the ships their. This was called 'Singeing the King of Spains beard'. Drake was* (55) *knighted by Queen Elizabeth and he became Sir Francis Drake. All these things made relations between England and Spain bad. In 1585 war broke out between them and in 1588 the Armada set out.*

2(b). CHANGES IN AGRICULTURE

The changes in farming methods brought a lot of advantages but they also had some disadvantages. (60)

The enclosures stopped diseases spreding in the animals and helped to get larger pigs, sheep and cows for food. But lots of the people who had owned strips lost out and ended up with either no land or poor marshy land outside the enclosures.

The new 'Norfolk' crop rotation produced more food which was (65) *needed for the growing towns. The turnips which were grown in the 'Norfolk' system were used to feed the livestock in the winter. This meant that the animals did not all have to be killed in the autumn and fresh meat was available in the winter.*

The new methods of planting seeds and threshing meant more corn to (70) *feed the people. But with all these new methods less people were needed so there was less employment and people had to move into the towns.*

For people who did find work in the enclosures the wages were good. The conditions in an enclosed village were better than they had been in (75) *the old villages.*

There were not too many disadvantages in the changes. Most of the changes were for the better.

Year 3: Two Examples of John's Work in English and Geography

3(a). THE CASE FOR AND AGAINST BLOOD SPORTS

Fox-hunting, hare coursing, grouse shooting, badger baiting and otter hunting are all blood sports. Many people are absolutely against it, (80) *but others say that it is reasonable and that it controls the species and keeps the numbers down.*

Arguments used by people who are against these sports are that they are bloody, cruel and inhumane. Hare coursing is often in the news. Hares are frightened out onto an open piece of land where two (85) *greyhounds are 'slipped' and they race after the hare when it is caught the hare is killed by them. The hare squels with fright and pain and often the dogs have a bloody tug of war with the live hare.*

Fox-hunting is often picketted by Anti-blood sport demonstrators. Grown men chase a fox to its death with hounds and the fox's den is (90) *staked up so he cannot escape.*

These sports are unnecisary, they can make the animals an endangered

species, say the people opposed to them, they are killing of British
wildlife.

People who aren't against the blood sports say they are perfectly   (95)
reasonable and justifiable. The sports get rid of pests who destory
crops and steal chickens, they are more humane than shooting hares
and foxes as the animal can get wounded by a bullet and escape to die
in pain. The greyhounds in hare coursing, say the people for blood
sports, are experts, a hare is killed swiftley and painlessly.   (100)
Anyway, as few as one in ten hares can be killed at a hare coursing
meeting.

I don't like blood sports. I think they are unnecisary, but where do
you draw the line? Not many people object to fishing, or to animals
being slaughtered for meat.   (105)

3(b). THE PROBLEMS OF LARGE MODERN CITIES

Large Modern Cities have many problems.

One problem is housing. Many people live in slums where the living
conditions are awful. Slum-clearance is an answer to the problem. The
buildings are demolished and the people rehoused in high-rise flats.

Because the factories are moving out of the city centre employment   (110)
has become a problem. Jobs for the unemployed can be created by the
government but welfare benefit is a more usual solution.

The concrete jungle of the skyscrapers, car parks and flats has become
as eyesore. The visual environment can be improved by government
planning making new buildings blend in with its background.   (115)

Food, fuel and water supplies for the cities are also a problem. Scien-
tists are inventing new scythetic foods which are cheaper and easier to
produce. New power plants and dams are being constructed to supply
power for the cities.

Transportation is another problem, there are far too many cars in the   (120)
cities. One solution is too build freeways and pedestrian precincts but
often the freeways encourage more motorists onto the roads. Some
People think that a monorail network should be built, like in Japan.

Pollution from traffic, sewage and factories is a big problem and the
government has brought in a new standards to reduce pollution.   (125)

There are many social problems in large modern cities, poverty, drugs,
crime and racial conflict. But the money is not available to solve these
problems.

Some people think there is nothing can be done about cities but I think
cities should be cleaned up and rehabilitatd.   (130)

Year 4: Two Examples of John's Work in Sociology and Chemistry

4(a). WHICH THEORIES DO YOU THINK GIVE THE BEST EXPLANATION FOR THE HIGH RATE OF JUVENILE CRIME IN CERTAIN PARTS OF LARGE CITIES, SUCH AS LONDON?

In my opinion the theory that best explains the reasons why certain parts of large cities such as London have a high rate of juvenile crime, is the theory of 'The Criminal Area'. In some part of large cities there is usually quite a lot of bad housing and poverty, and there is also quite a lot of unemployment. The part of this theory that I think (135) *might be a key factor in explaining the high rate of delinquency is that part that deals with ATTITUDES AND VALUES. The people in most large cities are used to high crime rates and are not so against crime and willing to help the police as people in other areas.*

The other sociological theories - Sunderland's and the theory of (140) *'Anomie' - would also help to explain why big cities have such a high rate of juvenile crime. Juveniles may receive less 'definitions unfavourable to crime' than definitions favourable to crime. Also the poverty in big cities would lead to people who wanted to achieve success using criminal means when they could not achieve their 'goals' by* (145) *the correct means - as in the theory of 'Anomie'.*

I don't think that the physical theories about individuals can explain the big cities' problems at all. I know that there are not lots of people in big cities with small skulls, big ears, thin upper lips etc so I don't think Lombroso's theories are correct. (150)

The Freudian theory could not explain the high rate of juvenile delinquency in cities either because there does not seem to be any reason why there should be more people who have not developed a 'superego' in big cities than in any other area.

The learning theories could explain high crime rates somewhat, (155) *because of the poverty in some big cities so that people steal so they can get a 'reward'. The part of these theories that could also explain it is the part relating to the family. Broken families are one of the social problems in big cities so juvenile delinquency might appear more. But I still think that the best explanation comes from that of the 'criminal* (160) *area'.*

4(b). THE MOVEMENT OF BROMINE MOLECULES IN AIR

In this experiment we used Bromine as it showed up easily because of its brown colour.

First of all we poured a few drops of Bromine from a bottle into the bottom of a glass jar (gravity pulled the Bromine down, bromine is (165) *heavier than the same amount of air.) We quickly covered the top of the glass jar with a cover glass. Then we got another gas jar filled with air and placed it over the top (a).*

(the writer adds his own diagram of the two glass jars)

When the cover glass was removed the brown bromine gas moved up and mixed throughout the two jars (b). The bromine moved quite (170) *quickly up to the top and, although we couldn't see it, air probably moved down into the bottom jar.*

This experiment shows us that the molecules of bromine are moving about, it is quite likely that the molecules in other gases move in the same way. (175)

The process of molecules moving as in this experiment is called diffusion.

Year 5: Two Examples of John's Work in English Literature and History

5(a). DISCUSS THE CHARACTER OF JIM AS PORTRAYED IN THE FIRST HALF OF THE NOVEL (HUCKLEBERRY FINN)

The character of Jim is in many ways quite remarkable in view of the situation he has been born into: being a negro slave in the southern states was a hard life, but Jim has managed to cope with it well. (180)
The first aspects of his character is that he is simple-minded. This is obvious in the way that he is deeply superstitious - he believes in witches, spirits and all kinds of signs of good and bad luck. Another way in which Jim is simple is when they argue about the story of King Solomon. Jim does not see that King Solomon's threat to cut the child (185) *in half was only a ploy to discover the true mother and he takes it literally. Jim is also very stubborn once he has stated his point of view. This is shown after the argument when Huck says to himself:*

> *'I never see such a nigger. If he got a notion in his head once, there warn't no getting it out again.'* (190)

The fact that Jim is gullible enough to believe that the two frauds are really the Dauphin and the Duke of Bridgewater is another indication of his simplicity. However this is only to be expected as Jim has had no education whatsoever, even Huck is more educated than him.

The second thing about Jim is that he is pragmatic, that is to say he is (195) *very adept at adapting to changing circumstances around him. Examples of this appear frequently throughout the novel: Jim's escape is a prime example, he escapes without help and remains level-headed throughout. He does not get frightened in a crisis, but keeps his cool, as he did when they get run down by the steamer and he escapes but* (200) *does not panic and cry out because of the danger of being caught and taken back into slavery.*

One exception to his level-headedness is when he and Huck are aboard the wrecked 'Walter Scott' and they find their raft is missing,

> *'Oh my lordy, lordy, Raf'? Dey ain' no raf' no mo', she done* (205)
> *broke loose en gone! - en here we is!' - says Jim.*

Jim is also a survivor who manages to live as one with nature when living on Jackson's Island and while travelling down river on the raft with Huck. His adaptability can be seen when he and Huck first get on the raft and he converts it by building a wigwam on it and makes a (210) *spare oar in case one were to get broken.*

Optimism is another quality which Jim is blessed with. An example of this is when he and Huck meet on Jackson's island and talk, Jim says:

> *No, but I been rich wunst, and gwyne to be rich agin.'*

In fact he only had fourteen dollars. Later in the same scene he gives (215) *an even better example of his optimism:*

> *'Yes - en I's rich now, come to look at it. I owns mysef,*
> *en I's wuth eight hund's dollars.'*

Another side of Jim's optimism is his trust. He says to Huck that he is the only white man he could trust. And his trust pays dividends when (220) *Huck proves himself trustworthy by not giving Jim away to the two men who are looking for runaway slaves (Chapter 16).*

Jim is also a very sensitive person and gets deeply upset when Huck plays a trick on him after they have got separated in the fog. Jim tells Huck: (225)

> *' 'En all you wuz thinkin' 'bout wuz how you could make a*
> *fool uv ole Jim wid a lie. Dat truck is trash; en trash is what*
> *people is dat puts dirt on de head er dey fren's en makes 'em*
> *ashamed.' '*

Lastly, an important emotion of Jim's is gratitude. He thanks Huck (230) *and is very grateful that he has helped him to escape. When they are nearing Cario he says to Huck:*

> *'Pooty soon I'll be a shout'n for joy, en I'll say, it's all on*
> *accounts o' Huck; I's a free man, en I couldn't ever ben*
> *free ef it hadn't ben for Huck. . . .'* (235)

Overall Jim is a very good person who does not harm anyone. Perhaps the fact that he is good could be due to his simplicity.

5(b). IN WHAT WAYS AND WITH WHAT SUCCESS DID (a) LENIN AND (b) STALIN ATTEMPT TO PROMOTE ECONOMIC GROWTH IN RUSSIA?

When the Bolsheviks came to power in November 1917, under the leadership of Lenin they wanted to get Russia to produce more. The

first of Lenin's policies was known as 'War Communism'. They seized (240)
land from private owners and the church to share amongst the
peasants. A commission was set up to plan the economy. All means of
production, agricultural and industrial, banking and foreign trade
were nationalised.

However these communist measures were forced onto the Russian (245)
people too quickly. In 1918 there was chaos, with the economy in
ruins, bad food shortages and the Bolsheviks printing banknotes.
They had to requisition grain and direct labour to where it was need-
ed.

The next policy which Lenin brought out was in 1921, after the Civil (250)
War. The 'flash that lit up reality', the Naval revolt at Kronstadt had
revealed to Lenin the dangers of the situation (March 1921). The New
Economic Policy (N.E.P.) first appeared in 1921. In it concessions
were made to capitalism. Peasants were allowed to sell crops and a
new class of wealthy peasant, the kulak, grew up. Pay incentivies were (255)
introduced for factory workers and some firms denationalised.

The economic policies under Lenin were not all that successful, by the
time Stalin came to power in 1928 Russia still had a production level
of 1914.

Stalin said, 'We are 50 or 100 years behind the advanced countries. (260)
We must make good this gap in 10 years. Either we do this or they
crush us.' Stalin's policies were nearly all successful, although strict,
and by the time of his death in 1953 Russia had made good the gap
and become one of the most industrially advanced countries in the
world. (265)

When Stalin came to power his aims were to increase food production
(to feed the new workers who were rapidly moving into the towns and
to export in order to buy machinery), to develop heavy industries, im-
prove transport systems and make Russia self sufficient in case of at-
tack from the capitalsit countries. This was to be done by a series of (270)
'Five Year Plans' organised by GOSPLAN, the state planning com-
mission.

In the first of these plans (1928 - 33) he abolished all free trade and
private wealth became state property. The government was to set pro-
duction targets, wages and prices. Much effort was concentrated on (275)
heavy industry, such as oil (Baku), steel production (Magnitorsk),
Hydro-electric power (Dnieper Dam), Agricultural machinery (trac-
tors), transport (railways) and coal production. In agriculture 70 - 100
families had to group together to form a collective or KOLKHOZE.
In this they pooled together their resources and were paid on the (280)
amount of work they did. 100 000 kolkhozee replaced 25 million

private farms. The government would buy grain and livestock at fixed rates (low).

However this plan was unsuccessful and caused a fall in production and food shortage, Russia had to import grain. This was due to the (285) *Kulaks opposition, they smashed ploughs, burnt crops and killed cattle. Stalin sent out his troops and 10 million Kulaks were 'liquidated'.*

In the second of these plans (33 - 37) Stalin was forced to compromise slightly, as Lenin had been with the N.E.P. Workers were given piece rates and incentives and factories were put in competition. Workers (290) *were encouraged to follow the example set by Alexy Stakhanov a coal worker who moved four times his usual amount of coal in one shift. In agriculture peasants were allowed 2½ acres of private land and a house of their own. They could sell any surplus grain for profit.*

Under Stalin welfare services such as a health service, unemployment (295) *and sick benefits were given to the people. Free schooling was introduced with a special look to science education. Illiteracy was reduced.*

To stop strikes which would hold up production the Trade Unions were state controlled. All capital was ploughed back into industry so (300) *living standards were low. Slacking, absenteeism, frequent change of job were forbidden by law - SABOTAGE AGAINST THE STATE, so was failing to meet production targets. People were encouraged to give their all for the community.*

The third five year plan 1937 - 41 was to have been given to the pro- (305) *duction of more consumer goods but war broke out and all efforts had to be concentrated on armaments.*

In looking at these essays, our procedure will be as follows:

1. We will look first, at the fifth year essay in English literature, on *Huckleberry Finn,* using that as the basis for spelling out the underlying formal structure of discursive writing.
2. Having looked at its structure, we will then evaluate its writing.
3. We will then use the same structure and evaluation as a basis for comparing all the essays.
4. In our concluding section, we will briefly summarize the developments in the boy's writing.
5. In addition, we will look at some of the implications for the teacher, and will also refer to the short stories looked at in the previous chapter.

The Formal Structure of Discursive Writing:
The Essay on Huckleberry Finn (Year 5)

In summary, our contention is that the essay shows an underlying structure of:

1. *Orientation* - enabling the reader to locate himself or herself in the general subject-matter and purpose of the essay;
2. *Strategy* - the plan of campaign by which the writer will set about the task;
3. *Evidence* - the organizing of various points and ideas to enable the strategy to be carried out;
4. *Conclusion* - establishing that the task is completed;
5. *Postscript,* and *coda* - qualifying the conclusion, indicating possible further strategies and further evidence

Orientation

The opening paragraph of the Huckleberry Finn essay, neatly brings the writer and the reader to the topic and task. We are told the kind of person Jim is, 'in many ways quite remarkable', and then given three absolutely essential facts about him, all in the same sentence.

Strategy

He then proceeds, without any kind of breather, to establish his strategy for exploring more precisely the character of Jim - 'The first aspect of his character is. . . .' In other words, he is going to select the major qualities of the man, and will elaborate upon them - 'This is obvious by the way that. . . .' (line 181). Interestingly, he does not spend time telling us that this will be his strategy, but there is, of course, no reason inherently why this specific strategy should be chosen, even though it is a very good one and he handles it well. He could have chosen to tell the story and to extract from the sequence of events the main qualities of Jim's character. He could have chosen to collect the principal events in Jim's career and examine them closely. He could have chosen to concentrate on the other characters and their response to and interaction with Jim. Instead, he chooses to extrapolate Jim's main qualities and construct his thinking around these. This means that he, to some extent, uses the other strategies we have just mentioned, but only marginally. It means too, that he has imposed a strategy which demands massive thinking *before writing.* He has to do a number of things. First he must decide that there are a definite number of distinct central qualities to Jim's character; in doing this, he must range through the novel, selecting the events which reveal these qualities. He has to eliminate ideas that are not substantiated by the text (or else, after writing down any such idea, withdraw it - which is something he does not actually have to do in the essay reproduced here); and also bring together events from different parts of the novel, which support the chosen idea.

Quite possibly this particular strategy involves more preliminary work, planning and thinking through, than some other strategies might, and this is something which the teacher can perhaps help the intending writer to do. But it is important to note at this point that any strategy requires preliminary working through, whether by way of taking notes, discussing or making rough drafts, or by all three. Some such activity is essential.

Evidence

In pursuing his strategy he is very adept at indicating the evidence for the various points he makes. At one stage (line 222) he refers to a specific chapter. He also quotes from the text, though without identifying precisely where the quotes occur. He illustrates all his major points, and, on one occasion underlines a major qualification of a point he has just made, when (line 203) he suggests that Jim's level-headedness is not absolute. The links between one point and the next are mostly made by simply numbering them 'first', 'the second thing' and so on. At one point he writes, 'One exception . . .' but elsewhere, 'Another side . . .' or, 'another quality. . . .'

Conclusion

John's essay arrives at its pre-stated conclusion, but with a slight variation. John began by writing that Jim is, 'in many ways quite remarkable' and then proceeds to elaborate on this. He concludes by writing 'Overall Jim is a very good person . . .' though he does not really explain why. He leaves that as something that is implicit in what has gone before.

Postscript

He also proceeds briefly to qualify his conclusion, noting, 'Perhaps the fact that he is good could be due to his simplicity.' This links to his first point about Jim's simplicity, while also leaving open the possibility of further thoughts on the subject.

We can now look at the essay as a whole.

Evaluation of the Huckleberry Finn Essay

The Writer's Thinking

Probably the most impressive aspect of the writing is the constant bringing together and then taking apart again of *the parts and the whole of the novel.* John is able to pick his way, backwards and forwards, through the narrative itself in order to find continuing threads, and then also to join these threads together to form a further central interpretation. This is even more impressive when one considers the sheer length of the novel itself, the range of incidents and the range of ideas running through them. There is at no point in the essay, any sense of the writer having lost his way through the novel, or of being unable to keep in mind what has gone before and what is to follow. There is, to the contrary, a remarkable sense of his being able to move around comfortably through, what could be, a maze of distinct, unconnected episodes and themes. In its own way, the essay is a good example of sustaining *the tension between* the part and the whole, and this tension is itself a part of all thinking, but not often as clearly so as it is here.

There are also certain links that he does not explore. In his analysis of the relationship between Huck and Jim, he does not note that Huck is conscience-stricken at helping a runaway slave. In conventional moral terms, Jim is a criminal offender of the highest order, and his goodness is not apparent to Huck in the early stages of the novel. Indeed, his coming to comprehend Jim's morality, is part of Huck's education.

What about the *economy and precision* of his thinking? He presents certain points as being linked generically, but without showing what the link really is. Thus trust is presented as another side of optimism (line 219) and stubbornness and gullibility are presented as facets of simple-mindedness (lines 187 and 193) which is probably correct, but the points need a little elaboration. He could have suggested how and why these qualities are complementary to one another. Elsewhere, he is very precise indeed, explaining what he means by pragmatism before going on to illustrate it. He is consistently economical - there is no repetition, not even a summing-up which simply restates what has gone before.

One weakness is that he does not actually *define* or even discuss the particular way in which he uses the concept 'character'. He takes it for granted that character is equal to the sum total of aspects. But aspects of what? - of character, presumably. He never explains. Had he done so, he might have considered other ways of defining the concept, and this might well have helped him to broaden his thinking.

A second possible weakness is that he does not invite himself to *qualify* his own interpretations. Jim is 'simple-minded' and then he gives examples of this simple-mindedness. This is fine, but it would be even better if he then asked - 'But is he really? Is he always?' Are there possibly some instances in the text where he shows an opposite quality? And if there are not, does this say anything about the character or about the writing? The one exception is when he qualifies Jim's level-headedness by reference to his behaviour on losing the raft. But this, interestingly, is not quite an example of what the writer suggests - it is not a lack of self-control so much as the very natural exclamation of concern in the face of disaster (line 203).

The writing is consistently *correct,* able to sustain the whole idea of writing discursively about the novel within the strategy that he employs, but it is at the same time *creative*. There is no sense of the writer being unable to express himself, or simply reproducing received opinion or a textbook's notes. Nor does he resort to critically fashionable clichés. He can write of Jim living 'as one with nature' (line 207) and being 'blessed with' optimism and his trust paying dividends.

Knowledge Used

The writer draws on two kinds of knowledge: of the novel itself, and of his own everyday knowledge of the way people behave. He makes major *assumptions* in his use of both. The two are brought together right at the beginning with the claim that Jim is 'remarkable in view of the situation he has been born into. . . .' This is not the view of Jim that is entertained by any of the characters in the novel itself, though Huck, very tentatively and falteringly, moves towards this view eventually. Even then, Huck would never see Jim as 'remarkable' without also offering a number of substantial reservations. The verdict is the writer's, John's, to some extent picking up the unstated tune of the author's, Mark Twain's, but largely rooted in John's own knowledge of the everyday world. For a man subjected to the stresses and strains of a slave's existence, Jim is a marvellously impressive human being. He deploys the same knowledge when he later comments that Jim's simplicity 'is only to be expected as Jim has had no education' (line 193). It is a knowledge rooted in massive assumptions which he does not feel at all impelled to articulate: the connections between education and simplicity (or the lack of it), and between slavery and character, are not explained. The writer sees these as too obvious to need stating. In effect, he sees himself and his reader as having already agreed on them.

Similarly, his use of the text is remarkable for what he is able to *leave out* from his writing. He again assumes a reader with an extensive knowledge of the novel, and indeed if he did not do so, he would be obliged to give extensive summaries of the plot every time he makes a point. For example, the important reference to the Dauphin and the Duke of Bridgewater does not explain their function in the story (line 192). Nor does he present the various illustrations from the plot in any kind of sequential order. If he did, he would again make a massive, and perhaps impossible, task for himself. This sense of what he does not need to say is absolutely central. It enables him to present in no more than a few hundred words a sequence of idea representing his response to a vast piece of literature. His primary source material is the novel itself, running into more than 100 000 words. Knowing how far he is to go in representing the novel and what he can leave out is a sophisticated and difficult exercise unto itself. Broadly, the rule of thumb which he appears to follow is that the bold outline of information relevant to a point is all that he has to spell out. He can take it for granted that the reader will then fill in the gaps.

He excludes certain areas of knowledge which could be seen as *relevant* to the subject-matter, and to which he probably has some access. There is no historical or moral comment on slavery. There is no other literary knowledge deployed: the writer does not refer to any similar character in other fiction or any similar work. This, again, is not to suggest he should do so, simply to indicate that there are other ways of thinking which he does not pursue.

He also excludes any explicit use of his own experience of the everyday world. He does not explain Jim's character in any relationship to real people he has known, or to people he has heard or read of. Nor does he in any way offer comparisons with himself. He does not say, for example, 'If this had happened to myself I would probably have. . . .' Indeed, if he had done so, he would almost certainly have departed from what he sees, probably correctly, as the conventional demands of the literature essay.

Language Used

Following on from the point we have just made, is the fact that the writer is very much in command of the *register* in which he is working. He keeps strictly to the text in front of him, writes impersonally, and sustains the use of the present tense as a means of reporting the various events of the story. This is of course not the only possible register in which to write literary criticism, but it is clearly the one in which he is writing here.

There are other important features of the language he uses. One is the absence of slips of any kind, whether of spelling or punctuation. Another is the complexity of the grammar of some of the sentences and their length. He is able to punctuate these sentences without difficulty, using colons and dashes, for example. He is able to place extensive quotations at the ends of his sentences without losing the sense of the introductory statement or of the quotation.

He has access to an extensive vocabulary for his enumeration of the varied aspects of Jim's character: simple-minded; superstitious; stubborn; gullible; pragmatic; adept, adapting; level-headed; adaptability; optimism; trustworthy; sensitive; emotion; gratitude; grateful; good.

Finally, it is a remarkable full-length piece of work, though not literally the longest of all the essays. Through some half a dozen or so paragraphs, the writer makes a sequence of points all supporting a single, central idea, and each point is itself briskly but meaningfully explored.

These, then, are the general features of this particular essay. We can now look across the whole range of his essays in this 5-year period, and begin to suggest what kinds of development seem to be taking place.

Kinds of Development in the Essays

The Writer's Thinking: Discursive Form

Whereas in John's story-writing he showed a clear command of the underlying structure of narrative right from the start of his secondary school career, this is not quite the case in his discursive writing. There is, in each case, a capacity to establish and hold on to a *strategy* around which his thinking revolves. He always sees this as a strategy imposed by the very nature of the task, as defined in the title of the essay. There is no sense of his choosing one strategy rather than another, and of his justifying his choice.

He does not really *orientate* his reader until he is writing in his third year. The first essay opens with - 'In the year 4000 . . .' which broadly sets the stage for the points he is about to make. In the second essay of the same year, the title is taken as being self-explanatory. And the same is true when we come to the second year essays. The essay on the Spanish Armada (2(a)) does not set the scene with an explanation of the Armada itself or of its historical context. We are taken straight into the three main reasons. Similarly, the next essay (2(b)) offers no kind of orientation in respect of the historical period in which agricultural changes are to be discussed or of the prevailing agricultural patterns of the time. Indeed no time is ever specified.

The first essay in the third year shows a clear development. The writer begins by giving examples of blood sports before proceeding to explain that some people are for them, others against. He then moves on to his strategy, which is to elaborate on the popular arguments of both sides. The other third year essay (3(b)) has an introductory statement which repeats the title of the essay, but there is no attempt to introduce the reader to the idea of large modern cities or to the ways in which they, in particular (unlike say, ancient large cities), are prone to problems, or to the kinds of problems to be considered. The same is true with both essays in the fourth year. Essay (4(a)) plunges the reader straight into the writer's view of the best applicable theory without setting the scene in relation to juvenile crime in cities, or in relation to what kinds of theories he is to consider and what he takes a theory to mean in any event. The second essay, (4(b)), follows the pattern of his first year essay on the evaporating of tap-water, and takes its title as self-explanatory. In the fifth year, he briefly but effectively orientates his reader to understanding the central factors of Jim's background (essay 5(a)) from which an elaboration of his character can be seen to make sense, but in the second essay, on Lenin's and Stalin's economic policies, there is virtually nothing to locate the reader in the particular historical context of the Bolshevik Revolution and its economic implications.

In all of the essays he arrives at some kind of explicit *conclusion,* where he effectively declares he has fulfilled the given task by the particular strategy he has chosen. The one exception is the short piece of writing in the first year, on the future, where he has clearly not seen the task as one of working out an overall picture based on specific details - hence there is nothing for him to conclude. But he always 'concludes' in all the other writing, across the five year period. In some instances he throws in the conclusion at the beginning (as in the fifth year essay on Huckleberry Finn) and sometimes introduces it in the middle of the writing - as he does with the other fifth year essay, where his conclusion on Lenin's policy (line 257) and then his conclusion on Stalin's (line 262) are less than half-way through the essay. This particular essay is much weakened by this lack of 'final' conclusion, as it were, for it remains questionable how far the evidence he has deployed does actually warrant the conclusion he has previously reached. He very much needs some brief résumé putting it all together in a way that demonstrates his central idea - that Stalin succeeded where Lenin failed.

He only twice employs any kind of *postscript* - in short, he only twice qualifies in any way his own conclusion. He does this in the third year essay on blood sports - 'I think they are unnecisary, *but* where do you draw the line? Not many people object to fishing . . .' (line 104). And he does it again at the end of the Huckleberry Finn essay - 'Overall Jim is a very good person . . . *Perhaps* the fact that he is good could be due to . . .' (line 236).

In short, he seems to have a clear sense, right from the beginning, of following through his strategy to reach a conclusion, but only irregularly does he see the need for further qualification of that conclusion. How does this variable command of the structural form, reflect itself in the quality of his thinking?

Economy and Precision

All the essays are economical, covering their territory, discharging the task in a very crisp fashion and engaging in little, if any, repetition. To some extent this is achieved at the price of exactness or precision. In this connection, the absence of a clear orientation in many of the essays is very relevant. The orientation serves an important function. It clarifies for the reader the central background information around which the essay is to be constructed, perhaps defining or explaining key terms employed. By its very nature, the orientation will be brief, but without it, rather too much may be taken for granted for the essay to stand on its own, and without it, the writer may never have to come to terms with the basic pieces of knowledge on which the essay is to be based. In this sense, from the writer's point of view, it may prove a serious omission. Nor are we confusing an orientation with an introductory flourish - this may be stylistically neat without in any way providing the reader with initial and basic information.

John proves himself capable of providing an orientation to his writings, doing this at different points in his career, in the third year and then again in the fifth year. He does not appear though, to have internalized this as a general technique. The consequence is that he does not, in general, *define* the key terms which he proceeds to use in his essays.

In the first year, he does not indicate the kind of world he is going to write about, whether the world of work, or transport, or food, or war, for instance. As a consequence, he very rapidly exhausts the range of his thinking, covering only food and travel. In the second piece of work for that year, he does not explain what he means by an experiment or what he means by evaporation, and this possibly relates to his making no attempt finally to evaluate the experiment itself.

In the second year, there is no attempt to explain what the Armada *is,* either in terms of the event itself, or, by analogy, with other such events. Similarly, there is no definition of the enclosure system in essay 2(b) or any elaboration of agricultural changes generally, and, as we have already noted, there is not even a specific declaration of the historical time under review. The first time he breaks this pattern is with his English essay, in the third year on blood sports, where he gives a fair number of illustrations of such sports from which, at least, a rough definition may be deduced (line 79). But this has not then become a general development, for in the geography essay for the same year, there is no attempt to enumerate the identifying characteristics of large modern cities, and again the overall quality of the writing suffers from this omission, for the various problems which he then goes on to enumerate are to a large extent random and arbitrary. Drugs and racial conflict, for example, have no explained connection with each other or with anything else. This could have been avoided had he made some attempt to explain how large modern cities have grown up, where and in response to what kinds of social and environmental conditions. The pattern continues in the fourth year. There is no explanation for instance, in essay 4(a), of what a theory is, whether generally or in sociology in particular, with the result that at least some of his evaluations of theories are not strictly evaluating what the theories set out to do. And, of course, none of the theories is actually explained or recapitulated. In the following piece of work, for science, there is no attempt to explain what a molecule is, or its relationship to air, and again no explanation of what qualifies as an experiment.

In the fifth year essay on Huckleberry Finn he takes the concept 'character' to be self-explanatory, though here the implication is quite well established - it is a collection of attributes deduced from a person's significant actions. In the next essay 5(b), there is no definition or explanation of any of the main concepts: Bolshevism, economic growth, economic policy, or capitalism, with again, fairly serious consequences for the quality of thinking with which these terms are deployed.

The Parts and the Whole

The creating of a discursive essay involves sustaining a line of thinking while constantly branching off to move from one point to another, utilizing all the evidence available. The risk is that the writer will lose the line of his or her thinking in these various different points, such that each point is more or less independent of the others. In other words, the parts may not add up to the whole.

The writer has, in some way, to spell out these various ways in which one part relates to another. Hence, *making clear the links* of the different stages of the discussion is absolutely essential. John seems able to do this, to some measure, even in his first year. He is assisted in his science writing by the very format of the writing itself: experiment, apparatus, and so on. This provides him with the headings around which to structure his thinking. The second year history essays both proceed coherently, the essay on the Armada, for instance, showing quite carefully how Mary's involvement with the Catholic problem in its turn involves her in the 'Spanish' problem, which is itself related to problems of commercial expansion internationally. Similarly, the third year essay on blood sports constructs itself around the basic cruelties of such sports and the possible justifications for them. The geography essay on large cities is a little less consistent. Some points are largely unconnected with one another - especially the sequence contained in the last few lines, while elsewhere point follows point clearly, as with his comment following the mention of slum clearance: 'Because the factories are moving out of the city centre employment has become a problem. Jobs for the unemployed . . .' (line 110).

In his fourth year sociology essay, he lists each theory in turn and briefly scores each one by his own criteria. And in the fifth year, in the Huckleberry Finn essay, he marks off one characteristic from the next very clearly, relating each in some measure to the other: 'The fact that Jim is gullible . . . is another indication of his simplicity . . .' (line 192).

In the history essay from the fifth year, the time sequence itself imposes the links from one point to the next, which thus becomes a variation of a narrative pattern - 'And then . . .' By following through with his task of noting the success or otherwise of those policies, he also creates a further link - that of rooting one policy in the success or failure of its predecessor: 'However this plan . . . caused a fall in production. . . . In the second of these plans (33 - 37) Stalin was forced to compromise slightly . . .' (line 288). Elsewhere in this essay, there are some quite arbitrary points. The connection between Stalin's welfare services and his economic policy, for example, is not explained (line 295). In other words, he sees the need to link his points quite early on, but again never internalizes this as an essential procedure: there is thus no simple linear development in this respect.

An important aspect of this whole business of linking one point to the next and to the overall line of the writer's thinking is the *qualifying* of points as they are made, of suggesting, 'But on the other hand . . .' or, 'Perhaps it could also be said. . . .' There are no such qualifications in John's work in the first year, but, in his second year history essay on the enclosure system, he very nearly qualifies his major (and erroneous) claim that 'there were not too many disadvantages in the changes . . .' (line 78) by adding that, 'most of the changes were for the better.' If he had made this qualification more explicit he would have arrived at a more accurate account of what happened. In his third year essay on blood sports, he shows himself well able to qualify one point with another. Each argument against, is countered by an argument for, without in any sense creating a mere list of unrelated ideas - '. . .but others say that it is reasonable and that it controls the species and keeps the numbers down . . .' (line 82). And the penultimate paragraph carries answers or counters to all the points made down to that point. It must be repeated that he has not simply given a number of arguments on one side and a number of arguments on the other (which is commonly done in all kinds of debate). He counters one argument with its qualification on the other side. This is well illustrated in his final paragraph - 'I don't like blood sports. I think they are unnecisary, but where do you draw the line? Not many people object to fishing, or to animals being slaughtered for meat.'

He does not, however, bring the same technique to bear in his other third year essay, in geography, on large cities. Here, his reluctance to qualify, leads him to a fair amount of contradiction, as when he comments on the unavailability of money to solve the city's problems and then adds that cities should be 'cleaned up and rehabilitatd' (line 130). Likewise, in his sociology essay in the fourth year, he fails to weigh one theory against another, in the way he has done previously regarding the arguments on blood sports, with the result that his selection of the 'best' theory is entirely arbitrary: 'But I still think that the best explanation comes from that of the 'criminal area' (line 160).

The same is true of the fourth year experiment with bromine: the brief demonstration of the movement of the molecules is accompanied by no consideration of any other possible interpretation. Even the major claim that the 'air probably moved down into the bottom jar' (line 172) is presented as self-evident. There is a brief moment of qualification in the essay on 'Huckleberry Finn' in the fifth year: 'One exception to his level-headedness is . . .' (line 203). And there is a similarly brief moment in the history essay (5(b)) when he comments that 'Stalin's policies were nearly all successful, although strict . . .' (line 262), but this essay, overall, has very little sense of qualifying major assertions with a view to showing the complexity of events. Thus, 'this plan was unsuccessful . . .' (line 284) and when 'war broke out . . . all efforts had to be concentrated on armaments . . .' (line 307). Similarly, the opening sentence, by failing to place economic policy, however briefly, within a broader social-political perspective, takes away the very factors with actually explain why the economic policies were only partially effective.

Correctness and Creativity

To what extent is he able to work expressively, creatively, within the constraints of the discursive form? In the second year, he can write, 'Francis Drake did all of these things and more' (line 48). In the third year essays 3, his final paragraph on blood sports is very much his own voice speaking, and the same is perhaps true of his comment on the Freudian super-ego in the fourth year sociology essay, at line 151. The fifth year essay on Huckleberry Finn has rather more creativity, a greater sense of being in command of his materials, rather than the reverse. Elsewhere, right across the essays, in the tension between being correct and being creative, the writing errs on the side of correctness. The writer is deliberately presenting information as correctly as possible and forsaking chances to fully engage himself, to follow through his points, to ask questions, to doubt. In this way, he keeps the discursiveness of what he writes in tight reins.

In short, the thinking behind his writing does not develop clearly or systematically from one piece of work to the next, or from one year to the next. There is a sense in which his thinking moves forward in one piece of work and then retreats in the next. How does this apply to the kinds of knowledge he employs?

Knowledge Used

Possibly the most striking single feature of this collection of essays is the sheer range of subject-matter they encompass, the constant accumulation of knowledge. Inevitably, this means that the writer is also making an increasing range of assumptions about what he does and what he does not have to write about, and similarly, is leaving out of his writing an increasing amount of what he knows, dismissing it as irrelevant.

Assumptions

In his first piece of work, on 'The Future', he is unsure of himself, not quite knowing what he is to think and write about, but when he writes in the same year about the evaporating of tap-water, he is much more aware of writing within a body of knowledge through which he is now beginning to chart his progress. In effect, what he writes is written entirely for one who knows all about it, and hence makes massive assumptions about what the reader already knows. There is no explanation, for instance, of the point of the whole exercise. By the second year this tendency is inevitably more pronounced: he knows more, and hence, assumes more of his reader. Thus, in the essay on the Armada, there is no explanation of the difference between a Catholic and a Protestant, whether on the purely religious level or the political level at the time. There is no explanation of the actual relationship, policital of personal, between Mary, Queen of Scots, Mary Tudor and Elizabeth Tudor. All this is taken for granted as knowledge shared by both the reader and the writer.

In his next essay, also in history, he, as it were, slips up on his assumptions, and in assuming that his reader knows a great deal of background information relevant to the enclosure system, forgets to mention the date, or even the historical period, in which the system occurred. In its way, this is a classic example of the difficulty for any student who realizes that some kind of assumptions have to be made, but does not have any guiding principle for determining which ones.

The same applies in the fourth year, where his sociology essay rests on the assumption that we (the writer and his reader) know what a theory is, and know all the specific theories employed in the essay. In the fifth year we have already noted the assumptions on which he builds his thinking about Huckleberry Finn - assumptions about the novel and about human nature. Similarly, in the essay on Russian economics, there is no explanation of Bolshevism in general or of its economic implications. The understanding of these is taken for granted.

Relevance

In his first year writing, it is clear that he is largely over-awed by the knowledge that he is writing *science!* He takes an exceedingly narrow view of what he can explore as part of the topic - 'The Future.' There is no fantasy, no science fiction, and little in the way of looking around his own everyday world and transplanting it into another world. Similarly, in the second year, he takes a confidently narrow view of the knowledge that is relevant. There is no use of general knowledge, of knowledge of modern events in any way parallel to the Armada, and no use of any kind of personal knowledge. For instance, he does not identify the Armada as a fearful experience for Elizabethans, analagous, say, to modern fears of nuclear warfare. He sees himself limited to a number of detailed facts which need no arguing or supporting evidence, and no relating to anything else.

He again omits whole areas of his own knowledge when he comes to write on blood sports in the third year for his English teacher. His view of what is relevant to the task proves to be highly exclusive - there is no use of fiction or films, or documentary programmes on TV, no use of poetry he has read, no kind of personal experience. He sees the form in which he is working as imposing a remarkably limited and impersonal range of experience, and this of course limits his performance, while also giving him a fairly firm territory on which to work. He approaches his geography essay, on large cities and their problems, in the same way: there is no insight into his own personal experience; no use of fiction; no use of the media; and interestingly, there is very little use of geography itself - he does not, for instance, look at the city in its geographical context and then explore the ways in which certain problems are inherent in the basic geographical situation of any city. Thus, he is again conscientiously seeking to use some knowledge, not all his knowledge, and to work strictly within the knowlege that he deems relevant. And in this way, he helps himself, limits himself, and sometimes misinterprets what is and what is not relevant.

In his fourth year, his sociology essay leaves out any reference to the fact that he, himself, lives in just such an area as he is writing about, and also leaves out any exploration of his own experiences there. In his fifth year, he omits from the Huckleberry Finn essay any reference to history (he does not, for example, make any historical statement about the author, or the subject of the book) or to literature in general. And in the essay on Russian economic policies there is no examination of conflicting economic theories, such as Marx and Adam Smith, even though he is writing about these elsewhere in his work at the same time.

So, as the writer extends the range of his knowledge he becomes increasingly adept at organizing and classifying what he knows, and hence knowing what he can and cannot leave out on any particular occasion. Likewise, he is increasingly adept at knowing what he can and cannot take for granted. But as he does this, so he, from time to time, makes the wrong assumptions, and draws the line across his thinking too soon. In part he pays the price of being almost too efficient in his learning.

Language Used

John's written language shows two opposing developments. On the one hand he virtually narrows the range of registers in which he is working. On the other hand, he extends the length of his various linguistic units. In general, he is able to write at greater length, using an ever-widening vocabulary and creating more complex sentences, as he goes along.

Registers

In his first year, his very short attempt to write about the world in the future is not based on any clear model of writing. It does not move towards scientific reporting, or the thinking out, on a very personal level, of the various possibilities of the kind one would find in a journal or magazine. As if aware of the absence of any clear model for what he is doing, the writer has placed underneath the writing a narrow strip of drawing right across the page, showing his own brief sketched view of the city of the future. In this way, he seems to be taking as his model the kind of illustrated layout of basic information that he would find in a comic or magazine - but without taking it very far. In effect, he does not know, on this occasion, the formal conventions within which he is to work: he has no clear models to build upon.

His second piece of work in the first year is the exact opposite: here he has the formal layout of scientific reporting - the experiment identified, the apparatus, the method, results, conclusion and the accompanying sketch. The form is almost greater than the contents for there is very little in the way of elaboration.

His first history essay, in the second year, observes a different convention - that of listing the central points he is to make, at the beginning of the essay, and then developing each in turn. Interestingly, he uses this in the first essay (on the Armada) and then drops it for the second - where it would be equally useful in organizing his thinking. Nor does he use it in any later essay, even where again it might help him (as in the essays for geography and history in the fourth and fifth years). In both essays, 2(a) and 2(b), his concept of the conventional form of this kind of historical writing seems to be rooted in the rapid sequence of facts, presented without any identification of the sources of evidence used, and presented also as connected in a self-evident fashion. Thus, 'Philip of Spain, wanting to make England Catholic, asked Elizabeth to marry him. Elizabeth refused him, she had no intention of marrying anyone, let alone Philip, for he was Catholic. . .'

Both the third year essays are attempts at formal discursive writing, unaided by headings or sub-headings, sustaining an impersonal tone of impartiality and detachment. They are, in this respect, ventures into something that is formally and conventionally most difficult, for such conventions (as with his science experiments) give a clear structure and strategy around which the writer can set to work (and the reader also). In both cases he unexpectedly slips into a more personal style at the very end - but only briefly.

The sociology essay in the fourth year observes the same conventions, and it is possible that he would have been helped here to extend his thinking by some specific use of headings and sub-headings, such as:

1. What is a sociological theory?
2. Juvenile crime in large cities - some statistics
3. Leading theories of social behaviour - (a), (b), (c), (d)
4. Their relevance to juvenile crime in large cities - (a), (b), (c), (d)

His fourth-year piece of scientific writing (4b) follows the same conventional format as his first-year writing for science: identifying the experiment, the apparatus, the method, the results and the conclusion, together with accompanying diagram. For some reason he does not feel impelled to identify each of these with its own sub-heading, as he had done before. Possibly, he now feels that this particular convention is no longer appropriate or proper. Possibly, he is generalizing advice given in one subject across all kinds of discursive writing in all subjects.

He is able in both his fifth year essays to write at length, to achieve full development in the discursive form, still observing the convention of uninterrupted prose, without any kind of overt, graphic pointers or illustrations.

In effect then, as he progresses through the secondary school system, he increasingly masters the art of writing discursively without the support of 'conventional' devices such as headings, sub-headings, essay titles broken down into a sequence of sub-questions, or illustrations. The only time he accompanies his writing with any kind of impressionistic sketch of his own, is in the brief first piece of work, in science, on the future of the world. He also of course, uses specific headings throughout his work in science. For the rest, the writing is within very austere registers and conventions - no pictures, no headings, just continuous prose. It is worth noting that most of us, and in particular most children, do not often see *models* of such writing. and in popular newspapers and magazines they are conspicuous for their absence.

Errors and Mistakes

John's command of the written language is very good throughout. There are occasional spelling errors (more relatively at the earlier stages than later) and he has the occasional difficulty with punctuation, where he runs two sentences into one, and this happens about once or twice with virtually every piece of writing. But it is interesting that almost invariably he seems to be aware of the problem, for he mostly uses a comma where the full-stop is needed, and so is clearly seeking to make some kind of marker. (This happens for example in line 41, and 257.) There are some occasions where a comma is needed to avoid ambiguity or confusion and where he does not supply one (see lines 292, 295, 299). And there is one point where a colon is needed to introduce a list of items, or alternatively, some added phrase - 'such as . . .' (line 126). But such errors are the exception, not the rule, and by the fifth year he is remarkably skilful in his use of punctuation. He is able to employ correctly: colons, the single dash, brackets and single and double quotation marks. This possibly indicates a growing grammatical complexity within the sentences, and may be linked to the occasional linguistic confusion which surfaces in the third year: 'The visual environment can be improved by government planning making new buildings blend in with its background' (line 114). This appears again in the fourth year with the very ambiguous statement that, 'The people in most large cities . . . are not so against crime and willing to help the police . . .' (line 137). And a little later: 'The learning theories could explain high crime somewhat, because of the poverty in some big cities so that people steal so that they can get a 'reward' . . .' (line 157). Interestingly, this kind of linguistic muddle does not occur in the first two years, perhaps because he his not writing at quite such length, perhaps, too, because he is not venturing out into sentences as grammatically complex.

Length of Units

The essays themselves get longer. There is marked lengthening between the first and second year writings and then later between the fourth and fifth year essays. The sentences themselves become correspondingly longer and more complex. Thus in his third year he is able to write, 'Arguments used by people who are against these sports are that they are bloody . . .' line 83. And then in the fourth year 'The other sociological theories - Sunderlands's and the theory of 'Anomie' - would also help to explain why big cities have such high rate of juvenile crime . . . (line 142). And later: 'Also the poverty in big cities would lead to people who wanted to achieve success using criminal means when they could not achieve their 'goals' by the correct means - as in the theory of 'Anomie' . . .' (line 146). There is a great deal of similar complexity in his fifth year work: 'This is obvious in the way that he is deeply superstitious - he believes in witches . . .' (line 181). And in the history essay there is, for example, the lengthy list of Stalin's aims enumerated in one sentence, complete with a neatly bracketed aside (line 267).

As for the vocabulary, we have already noted the wide range of terms employed in the fifth year, in the essay on Huckleberry Finn. But it seems fair to say that in this respect his language always rises to the occasion, from his second year onwards. What is remarkable is the ability to meet the challenge across such a range of subject-matter. For example, his second year essay on the Armada employs a range of concepts concerned with power of one kind or another, including: Catholic; Protestant; make him her heir; under Spanish rule; rebelling; imprisoned; right to the throne; executed; treasure ships; slave trade; raiders or pirates; colonies; raiding Spanish ports; relations between England and Spain; knighted. His essay on blood sports is equally impressive in this respect (3(a)) as also is the third-year essay on city problems, where he is able to deploy a similarly wide range of concepts to explore the central theme of urban problems: slum-clearance; demolished and rehoused; high-rise; welfare benefit; government; concrete jungle; visual environment; government planning; synthetic foods; freeways and pedestrian precincts; monorail network; pollution; racial conflict, rehabilitated.

Summary

The Learner's Development

1. In some respects there is a much clearer development in John's discursive writing than in his story-writing. In particular, his command of the discursive form increases greatly from very modest beginnings. His development, though, is by no means consistent or comprehensive.

2. His actual thinking is variable. He is always economical, but not always precise, and in particular often fails to define what he writes about or to qualify the claims he makes. He is generally correct in representing the key information that he needs to handle and the ideas that he thinks are acceptable to make, but not generally creative: he does not often follow through his own line of thinking, ask his own questions, express his own uncertainties. He shows throughout, though, an ability to hold on to a range of evidence.

3. Possibly the most obvious development is in the sheer range of subject-matter with which he becomes familiar.

4. The more he 'knows' the more he is able to reject what he knows for any specific task, and thus to make major assumptions about what the reader needs to be told and what is and what is not relevant. Not surprisingly, this sometimes creates problems for him rather than solving them.

5. His language shows clear development in terms of range of vocabulary, length of essays and complexity of sentences. At the same time, the registers in which he writes, or more exactly, in which he is asked to write, seem to show a narrowing towards continuous discursive prose without any kinds of headings, sub-headings or illustrations.

6. In general, the clearest developments seem to occur between the first and second years, and between the fourth and fifth years.

We can now look, finally, at the implications of these developments in writing stories and in writing discursively for the teacher in the classroom. In so doing, we will briefly draw together some of the points we have previously made in relation to talking and reading, and so offer a short summary of the whole book.

Conclusions

Generalization about Language Development

All the evidence from John's writing, as quoted in the last two chapters, seems to indicate the danger of offering sweeping generalizations about a particular child's language development. The point is itself obvious enough, but also important. Major decisions about children's intelligence, aptitudes and careers are based on such generalizations. As John moves through his secondary schooling he shows a continuing capacity to make sense of a vast range of subject-matter, but the thinking he brings to these various tasks is very inconsistent. This is paralleled by the evidence of the children engaged in group discussions of excerpts from different kinds of literature, which we looked at earlier. Here a generalized statement that certain children could not cope with literature because of its inherent complexity, proved at times inaccurate. The children's ability depended on a small range of variables, including not only the language itself but also the kinds of knowledge involved and the particular way in which they were asked to work and the kinds of thinking that the work encouraged.

Ways of Thinking

In the case of John's writing, he greatly extends his knowledge in a great variety of fields and disciplines. Hence his work shows something of the imprint of very good teaching. At the same time he seems to have internalized an emphasis on getting things right, on writing what is expected of him, on getting the task over and done with. There is nothing perverse about this, or surprising. We have carefully stressed that all learning, and hence all teaching, involves different kinds of tension in which there is more or less bound to be a slight emphasis one way or the other - on creativity, for instance, as against correctness. In effect, John's writing (including to some extent his stories) shows a leaning towards economy rather than precision, and towards correctness at the price of creativity. With a child less successful, less adept than John, such an emphasis could well be fatal, inhibiting thought almost entirely, confusing the language that he or she uses, weakening what is already known.

In other words, whether we are talking of children as 'average' or 'above average' or what we will, there is a continuing need to place the emphasis, at least at certain times, on thinking things out, rather than getting things right. This may mean a number of things. It may mean spending time looking at what certain concepts mean, and talking and thinking about them in a leisurely fashion so that the learner has a chance to arrive at a more or less precise understanding. It may mean spending time while questions are asked by the learner and explored with other learners, not simply answered by the teacher. In this way, the learner approaches the topic creatively, personally involved, forging links with his or her own present experience. It may mean also, spending time looking into all those parts of the problem which the learner finds difficult, and which therefore elicit a fair number of his or her questions. In effect, at such times, there is a chance for the learner to put the parts before the whole, to look carefully at those particular trees that seem to impede the view of the wood.

Knowledge Used

Whenever we learn something we in various ways forge links between the familiar and the unfamiliar, between what we know already and what we are now learning. One of the problems of the learner is that what is new is always based on what is already familiar to others, and hence based on various major assumptions about what needs to be stated, explained, considered and so on. Children are likely to internalize these assumptions without knowing what they actually are assuming. In their writing they may display, as John does, what is virtually a convention of knowingness, of having access to experience which they in fact do not have, of knowing things they do not know. In other words, they make the wrong assumptions. The result is confusion, but it can be confusion masquerading quite successfully as well-organized thought, especially if the conventions of a particular register have been quite carefully internalized.

Once again, the children's own questions can play a major part in helping the teacher as well as the children to see what their assumptions are.

At the same time, learning something new involves not only forging links with what we know already but also putting to one side a vast amount of what we know already, judging it to be irrelevant. There is a fair amount of evidence in all the examples we have given in this book of children talking, reading and writing, that learners need help not to make such judgements too readily, that they need to be encouraged to open out the field of their inquiry at certain times rather than to narrow it down. In effect, the problem is not that the learner does not know, but that he or she does not realize how much is known and how relevant it is.

Language Used

John started his secondary schooling with an extensive ability to write stories. By contrast, his ability to write discursively was limited, and it was therefore within the discursive form that he made the more apparent, if irregular progress, in the next five years. One reason for this is the prevalence of *models* of the narrative form in his experience, not only in his earlier schooling but also outside the school, in his everyday life and in the media. Moreover, we have seen how the basic structure or form of narrative is the same, whether we examine oral story-telling or written story-telling. So the models he has heard and listened to, and has created for himself in gossip with friends, have also provided him with models for his story-writing.

By contrast, his experience of discursive talking and writing is likely to have been limited, whether at first or second hand. Yet the interesting thing is that the underlying form for both oral and written discursiveness is the same, just as it is for oral and written story-telling. When examining the group discussions earlier in the book we were able to identify the same structure of orientation, strategy, evidence, conclusion and postscript that we noted in the discursive writing. In other words, the learner's experience of talking discursively also provides him with models for writing discursively. The same formal structure applies.

At the same time, a wide experience of different registers in which, in one way or another, discursive writing is in evidence, will greatly influence the learner's own writing. One of the dangers is that the school will go too comprehensively for the kind of continuous prose-writing which typifies the writing of what we might call the professional philosopher, and leave out the use altogether of writing which uses headings, sub-headings, questions and illustrations as a means of clarifying for reader and writer alike the broad strategy which is to be adopted.

To help children internalize all the various registers which the school wishes them to employ, there is, of course, a lot to be said for making extensive use of children's own writing as models for other children. This may well help to clarify to children, and also to teachers, the scope as well as the difficulties of the particular conventions they are working with. Such models should include not only the kinds of finished products which we have been looking at, but also brief notes, and the listing of say, three or four points on each side of an argument, with a brief elaboration on each. There will be a special need for such introductory work in the early stages of the secondary school (and the later stages of the primary school) but there will be a general need for it at all stages of the curriculum.

Ways of Working

The idea of *models* is also pertinent when we come to the ways in which children are asked to work. Discussion, reading, talking and writing all belong together, offering complementary opportunities to the learners to extend their experience and understanding. But in order to work together in this way, in order to discuss things, whether as a small group or as a whole class, children need help to internalize the various conventions of discussion. Thus they need to discuss in order to learn how to discuss, but they also need to become interested in the idea of discussion itself, to think about its possibilities.

Discursive talking or writing is essentially improvisational, with the participants having to think on their feet, have their wits about them, and be prepared to shift their position. In this way it is more complex than most informative writing or talking, which is essentially a repetition of something already known and rehearsed. It is also more complex than the various forms of persuasive language, where the outcome, the conclusion, is similarly predetermined. It is probably as complex, in fact, as the uses of language that, especially in education, are widely termed creative, as with the writing of a play or novel. Because it is a form of improvisation, there is an important place in the class for all the different aspects of that improvisation, such as the making of notes, the writing of rough first drafts, the brief listing of points, the editing and revising of first drafts and recasting them as second or even third drafts, as well as the kinds of finished 'essays' which we have looked at in the previous chapter. Again we would stress that these embryonic forms of discursiveness may at certain stages be exactly what are needed - embryonic and no more.

So our intentions in the writing of this book lie in two slightly different directions, though both of them are concerned with the teacher in the classroom. On the one hand, we are keen to encourage certain techniques on the part of the teacher that seem to us to help children to learn. In effect, these are *classroom techniques* that focus on the four basic and related aspects of all learning - the kinds of knowledge used, the ways of thinking, the ways of working, and the language itself. Essentially, the technique of the teacher involves deliberately varying the work in the classroom so that by talking, listening, reading and writing, the learner can find ways of mastering what is new and what is difficult.

On the other hand, we are also keen to encourage procedures that go beyond the province of any individual teacher and hence pertain to *teaching strategies right across the curriculum.* One example of this would be the charting of the work of an individual child's work at a specific point in his or her education right across the school. A staff working party, for instance, might examine everything the child writes in a given week, or everything the child is asked to read. Another example would be developmental studies of a child's work, such as the work we have used in this book to explore John's writing over a 5-year period. One valuable by-product of such studies could well be an increased interest in maintaining some system for collecting examples of children's work as they progress through the school, so that there is always some means of comparing their work at different points in their schooling.

A second way of exploring and stimulating teaching strategies across the curriculum is by focusing on the activities of the teachers themselves. An example would be a study of all the kinds of writing engaged in by, say, a class of 12-year-olds in any given week, or of the amount of time devoted to reading and to writing and to talking. Equally valuable would be studies of the extent to which teachers engage children in making their own notes and of the techniques which they help children to use. Other examples would be studies of the kinds of questions children ask in lessons, with perhaps each teacher who takes a class in a given week, recording the questions actually asked by the children. Alternatively, a study might be made of the attempts of teachers to vary their own role in class discussion along the lines we have explored in Chapter 4: how easy or successful, for example, are attempts to remain impartial or non-committal?

Such studies must emanate from the teachers themselves, and perhaps in the first instance from small groups of teachers in just one or two departments. They are essentially exercises in self-observation and evaluation which can lead to a great sharing of ideas, and we feel that the model we have outlined in this book, or aspects of that model, can make a real contribution to the shaping of these ideas. In their turn, these ideas can make a major contribution to change and development in teaching practice.

One major problem of the curriculum is the sudden introduction of discursive writing as a major activity when the child is around the age of 12 or 13. There seems to us to be fairly little preparation for this, and thereafter there is very little in the way of revision of the preparatory stages. Also, children, who cannot produce discursive writing of a quite sophisticated kind, are then generally considered to be unable to think discursively at all. Our own argument is that teachers need a fairly wide-ranging perspective to see the different kinds of difficulties that children can encounter, and that they need to set up activities involving many different kinds of talking, listening, reading and writing to help children overcome these difficulties. This is essential not at any single stage of the curriculum but at all stages, and not for any one group of children but for all children, right across the curriculum.

Notes

In working out our ideas we have been influenced by a great variety of thinkers. Those of whose influence we are most aware are the following:

On the relationship of *relevance* to learning, A. Schutz, *Collected Papers,* Volume 1, part III (section on the Intersubjective World) and see also P. Berger and T. Luckman, *The Social Construction of Reality.* Both these works also discuss the role of *assumptions* in knowledge, and the ways in which all kinds of learning in effect build upon certain things which are taken for granted. This is explored also in Thomas Kuhn's *The Structure of Scientific Revolutions,* where the emphasis is on the ways in which changes in scientific theories have to overcome the adherence to long-standing (and of course unstated) assumptions.

On the idea of *precision* as a central feature of thinking, and thus of learning, J. Lyons, *Semantics,* Volume 1 (see especially page 49, where he writes about 'the elimination of uncertainty' as part of the making of meaning). And see, also, *Semantics* by Geoffrey Leech, especially the chapter on 'Seven Types of Meaning'.

On the idea of different levels of thinking, and of returning to familiar ideas at a more complex level, J. Bruner, *Towards a Theory of Instruction.* This is explored also in Margaret Donaldson, *Children's Minds.*

On the idea of *creative* as opposed to 'correct' thinking, see for example Edward de Bono, *The Use of Lateral Thinking.* See also Mike Torbe's useful distinction between language for communciation and language for learning, in his contribution to A. Cashdan's *Language, Reading and Learning.*

On the role of *conventions in talking,* Roy Turner, editor, *Ethnomethodology* (see Turner's own chapter on 'Methodical Bases of Interaction'). See also David Sudnow, editor, *Studies in Social Interaction,* especially Matthew Speier's essay, 'Aspects of Conversational Structure'. Also, J. Cook-Gumperz - her essay on 'Language Socialisation of School-Age Children' in *Child Discourse,* edited by Susan Ervin-Tripp.

On the role of *conventions* in all kinds of thinking, see for example, M. A. K. Halliday, *Learning How to Mean,* especially the final chapter, 'The Social Context of Language Development'. See also J. Britton, his essay in *Problems of Language and Learning,* edited by A. Davies.

On the difference between *spoken and written* language, see the essay by Geoffrey Roberts in *Language, Reading and Learning,* edited by Asher Cashdan; also Eric Lunzer, *Effective Use of Reading;* also J. Sinclair and R. Coulthard, *Towards an Analysis of Discourse.*

On the idea that language may be *'incorrect'* while also being perfectly *'meaningful',* N. Smith and D. Wilson, *Modern Linguistics,* especially the chapter on 'Types of Linguistic Knowledge'. See also Lois Bloom, *Language Development,* and her distinction between a linguistic grammar and a mental grammar.

On the different ways in which language may be complex, and the implications of this for the classroom situation, see Lunzer, *Effective Reading,* and Frank Smith *Reading,* and the same author's *Comprehension and Learning.*

On the use of *cloze reading tests,* Lunzer, *Effective Use of Reading,* and the same work for an account of the *Flesch* method of scoring the reading-difficulty of a given passage. For a further discussion of cloze tests, and of their limitations, see J. B. Carroll and R. Freedle, editors, *Language Comprehension and the Acquisition of Knowledge.*

On the *formal components of oral narrative,* William Labov and J. Waletzky, *Narrative Analysis,* in *Essays in the Verbal and Visual Arts* (June Helm, editor). The writers' analysis of the underlying form and structure of oral narrative is immensely interesting, and led us to our own attempt to explore the structure of discursive talk and writing in a similar way.

On the importance of the *child's own questions* to the work of the teacher, Frank Smith, *Reading,* and see also Bryant Fillion, *Reading as Inquiry: An Approach to Literature Learning.* (*English Journal,* January 1981, Volume 70.) Also the Bullock Report, *A Language for Life,* especially at page 118.

On the distinction between *cognitive and linguistic* development, J. Piaget, *Language and Thought of the Child,* and also Beryl Geber, editor, *Piaget and Knowing.* See also Margaret Donaldson's re-evaluation of Piaget in *Children's Minds.*

On the application of differing *models* to the *study of language development,* see for example, the discussion of Chomsky's reductionist model, Vygotsky's interactionist model, and Hymes' unified model, in M. Lewis and L. Rosenblum, editors, *Interaction, Conversation and the Development of Language.* For a detailed application of a quite different model to classroom learning, A. Wilkinson and others, *Assessing Language Development.* Equally fascinating is *The Carleton Writing Project,* a study of the writing abilities of children in Grades 5, 8 and 12, by Aviva Freedman and Ian Pringle.

On the *role of the teacher* in creating a good environment for learning, see O. Oeser and others, *Teacher, Pupil and Task;* Elizabeth Richardson, *The Environment of Learning;* and C. M. Fleming, *Teaching.* All these are concerned primarily with ways in which the teacher helps children to work together and thus to learn from and with each other.

On the *language of the classroom,* Connie and Harold Rosen, *The Language of Primary Schoolchildren;* also H. Rosen, J. Britton and D. Barnes, *Language, the Learner and the School.* More specifically on children *talking together,* and on the difference between class and group discussion, B. G. Massialas and H. Zevin, *Creative Encounters in the Classroom,* and Douglas Barnes, *From Communication to Curriculum.* A good general introduction to the whole relationship of talking to learning is given in *Understanding Children Talking,* by Nancy Martin and others.

On the *teaching of writing,* Nancy Martin and others, *Writing and Learning;* also Frank Smith, *Writing and the Writer;* and see also Janet Emig, *Non-Magical Thinking: Presenting Writing Developmentally in Schools.*

On the *teaching of reading,* we must mention yet again the work of Frank Smith and also of Eric Lunzer, referred to above.

Reading List

These are works which we have found especially helpful at various times:

General Background

Berger, P. & Luckmann, T. *The Social Construction of Reality*, Penguin University 1971
de Bono. E. *The Use of Lateral Thinking*, Cape 1967
Burke, K. *Language as Symbolic Action*, Univ. of California 1966
Goffman, I. *Interaction Ritual*, Allen Lane 1972
Kuhn, T. *The Structure of Scientific Revolutions*, Routledge and Kegan Paul 1968
Richards, M. P. M., editor, *The Integration of a Child into a Social World*, Cambridge Univ. 1974.
Schutz, Alfred, *Collected Papers*, Vol I, Nijhoff, The Hague 1971
Turner, R. editor, *Ethnomethodology*, Penguin 1974

Language and Learning

Bloom, L. *Language Development*, M.I.T. Press 1970
Britton, J. *Language and Learning*, Penguin 1972
Bruner, J. *Towards a Theory of Instruction*, Belknap Press, Harvard 1966
Carroll, J. & Freedle, R. O., editors, *Language Comprehension and the Acquisition of Knowledge*, Winston/Wiley 1972
Cashdan, A. editor, *Language, Reading and Learning*, Blackwell 1979
Crystal, D. *Child Language, Learning and Linguistics*, Arnold 1976
Dale, P. S. *Language Development*, Holt, Rinehard 1976
Davies, A. editor, *Problems of Language and Learning*, Heinemann 1975
Donaldson, M. *Children's Minds*, Fontana 1978
Edwards, V. K. *The West Indian Language Issue in British Schools*, Routledge 1979
Ervin-Tripp, & S. Mitchell-Kernan, C. *Child Discourse*, Academic Press, New York 1977
Freedman, A. & Pringle, I. *The Carleton Writing Project*, Carleton Univ. 1980
Gannon, P. & Czerniewska, P. *Using Linguistics: an Educational Focus*, Arnold 1980
Geber, B. *Piaget and Knowing*, Routledge 1977
Greene, J. *Thinking and Language*, Methuen 1975
Greene, J. *Psycholinguistics, Chomsky and Psychology*, Penguin 1972
Halliday, M. A. K. *Learning How to Mean*, Arnold 1975
Hanson, F. A. *Meaning in Culture*, Routledge 1975
H. M. Inspectors of Schools, *Aspects of Secondary Education in England*, H.M.S.O. 1979
Labov, W. & Waletzka, J. *Essays in the Verbal and Visual Arts*, June Helm, editor, Univ. of Washington Press 1967
Leech, G. *Semantics*, Pelican 1974
Lewis, M. & Rosenbaum, L. editors, *Interaction, Conversation and the Development of Language*, Wiley 1977
Lyons, J. *Semantics* (two volumes), Cambridge Univ. 1977
Marland, M. editor, *Language Across the Curriculum*, Heinemann 1977
Martin, M. *The Martin Report (What goes on in English lessons) Case Studies from Government High Schools in W. Australia*, Dept. of Education, W. Australia 1980
Piaget, J. *The Language and Thought of the Child*, Routledge 1959
Piaget, J. *The Moral Judgement of the Child*, Routledge 1932
Rosen, C. and H. *The Language of Primary Schoolchildren*, Penguin Education 1973
Sinclair, J. & Coulthard, R. *Towards an Analysis of Discourse*, Routledge 1975
Smith, N. & Wilson, D. *Modern Linguistics*, Penguin 1979
Stubbs, M. *Language and Literacy, the Sociolinguistics of Reading and Writing*, Routledge 1980
Sudnow, D. editor, *Studies in Social Interaction*, Collier-Macmillan, New York 1972
Trugdill, P. *Sociolinguistics, an introduction*, Penguin 1974

Wilkinson, A. and others, *Assessing Language development,* Oxford Univ. 1980
Winnicott, D. W. *Playing and Reality,* Tavistock 1971

Teaching-Strategies

Barnes, D. *From Communication to Curriculum,* Penguin Education 1976
Bullock Report, *A Language for Life,* H.MS.O. 1975
Dickinson, A. & Lee, P. editors, *History Teaching and Historical Understanding,* Heinemann 1978
Dixon, J. *Education 16-19, The Role of English and Communication,* Macmillan 1979
Doughty, P., Pearce, J. & Thornton, G. *Exploring Language* and by the same authors, *Language in Use,* Arnold 1971
Emig, J. *Non-Magical Thinking - presenting writing developmentally in Schools,* in 'The Nature, Development and Teaching of Written Communication', C. Frederikson, editor, Erlbaum, New Jersey, 1981
Filion, B. *Reading as Inquiry: an Approach to Literature Learning* English Journal volume 70, January 1981
Fleming, C. M. *Teaching,* Routledge 1959
Gatherer, W. A. *The Study of English: Learning and Teaching the Language,* Heinemann 1980
Keen, J. *Teaching English - a linguistic approach,* Methuen 1978
Lunzer, E. & Gardner, K. *The Effective Use of Reading,* Heinemann 1979
Martin, N. and others, *Writing and Learning across the Curriculum,* Ward Lock 1979
Martin, N. and others, *Understanding Children Talking,* Penguin Education 1976
Mackay, D. and others, *Breakthrough to Literacy,* Longmans 1970
Massialas, B. & Zevin, H. *Creative Encounters in the Classroom,* Wiley, New York 1967
Medway, P. Finding a Language - *Autonomy and Learning in School,* Writers and Readers 1981
Oeser, O. A. and others, *Teacher, Pupil and Task,* Tavistock 1962
Richardson, E. *The Environment of Learning,* Routledge 1966
Smith, F. *Comprehension and Learning* (Holt, Rinehard 1975) *Reading* (Cambridge Univ. 1978), *Writing and the Writer* (Holt, Rinehard 1971)
Thornton, G. *Teaching Writing,* Arnold 1980
Torbe, M. *Language Policies in Action,* Ward Lock 1980
Torbe, M. & Medway P. *Language and the Climate for Learning,* Ward Lock 1981
Tough, J. *Focus on Meaning,* Unwin 1973
Widdowson, H. G. *Teaching Language as Communication,* Oxford Univ. 1978

Index of Pupil's Activities